A PRACTICAL GUIDE

TRUTH
COUNTS

FOR NEWS CONSUMERS

Edited by Matt Mansfield and Ellen Shearer

President & Managing Director
Paul McHale

Editor-in-Chief
Kris Viesselman

Design Director
Marilyn Gates-Davis

Copy Editor
Lindsey Gilbert

CQ Roll Call 1625 Eye Street, Suite 200, NW, Washington, D.C. 20006-4061
info.cq.com, rollcall.com

ISBN: 978-0-9994368-4-4

Dedicated to

Steve Komarow

Contents

Foreword

The idea of truth has taken a beating since the 2016 presidential campaign. Truth itself soldiers on, of course.

Yet so much deliberately false information has made its way into, well, seemingly everywhere in American life that finding new frameworks for understanding and evaluation is essential.

Where to start though? Truth, it's apparent, has become increasingly difficult to tease out.

Look at your social media diet.

Consider the information you consume.

Take a stroll through your Facebook feed.

It's ugly out there — and it feels like it's getting worse. Because of the insular ways we can now self-select where we get news, where we find out what is true and what is not, our individual filter bubbles are in full effect.

Our social worlds, and thus often our belief systems, are contributing to a distance that feeds on itself. Can we ever understand someone with a view different from our own? Can we know if that view is true? Or whether we simply dislike it, despite its veracity?

Finding a way forward amid the misinformation, the fake news and head fakes, the endless cycle of Twitter memes and movements, is the best part of living in our current information age because we're equipped with all the tools we need to stay out of the dark.

So let's get started.

First, a word about the publishers of this book: It is natural for CQ to take on this thorny topic and contribute to the widening conversation about truth. It's in keeping with CQ's unparalleled role as a nonpartisan player.

"CQ is in the truth business," said Paul McHale, CQ's president. "I asked Ellen [Shearer] and Matt [Mansfield] to examine how CQ could help people understand the truth in this tremendously confusing time. Our promise to clients is 'Truth, Delivered' and they count on us for that. Readers of this book, I trust, will also see our value in this regard."

CQ, which is owned by The Economist Group, has a deep, well-deserved reputation, as McHale notes, for explaining the labyrinth that is official Washington: Congress, the

> *"CQ is in the TRUTH business."*

White House, agencies, lobbyists, think tanks, the advocacy industry and all the forces that contribute to federal rules.

Congressional Quarterly, as it was then known, was founded in 1945 by Nelson Poynter and his wife, Henrietta. They had a goal in mind. "The federal government will never set up an adequate agency to check on itself, and a foundation is too timid for that," he said. "So it had to be a private enterprise beholden to its clients."

Keeping a check on power, then, is officially in the DNA of CQ.

The media and legislative tracking company has enlisted an all-star roster of writers to look at the idea of truth in our time. These writers explore 10 different concepts and frameworks for finding the truth amid deliberate falsehoods, propaganda, partisan rhetoric and the nonstop cacophony enabled by technology.

Why do this? Everyone needs to know how to separate truth and facts from everything else; we need ways to test ideas. If you're having difficulty finding the truth or understanding which "fake news" isn't fake and which is, we hope this book will guide you.

We'll follow up throughout 2018 with podcasts and other digital (and IRL) conversations to consider truth ahead of the fall elections. We anticipate a great deal of fodder for this exploration.

We hope you will join us.

— Matt Mansfield and Ellen Shearer

CHAPTER ONE

Truth Matters

By
Tom Rosenstiel
and
Katherine K. Ellis

Daniel Patrick Moynihan

CQ Roll Call file photo

Truth Matters

When people today worry about the rise of misinformation and the prevalence of opinion mongering on cable television and elsewhere, they often quote the late Sen. Daniel Patrick Moynihan's line: "Everyone is entitled to his own opinion, but not his own facts."[1]

Oh, if the senator could only take it back.

Moynihan made the comment offhandedly in a television interview, not in a carefully written treatise, and there's a problem with his construction: While people are entitled to their own opinions, they are also entitled to select their own facts. Doing so is part of logic and argumentation.

The problem facing democracy in the 21st century — and with it the profession of journalism that helps make democracy possible — is larger and more serious than people being selective about their facts. It is a degradation of the idea that facts have meaning at all.

> *"Everyone is entitled to his own opinion, but not his own facts."*

We have reached a moment — in the shift from gatekeepers oriented around verification to information platforms built around connectedness and openness — in which the value of facts is unclear.

And rather than a more connected world, we are coming to grips with the realization that this new information landscape, in many ways, is merely another means of dividing consumers into markets, one that has less to do with geography and civic arrangements and more to do with passions, interests and beliefs.

A complex set of technological, political, economic and social factors have converged to contribute to this moment. The causes go well beyond the rise of platform companies, the disruption of the economic model of journalism and a more confrontational style of politics. But the risks to governing and democracy that have resulted are enormous.

We have seen the rise of actual fake news, as well as the labeling of objective information as "fake news," the growing spread of misinformation, the success of state-sponsored efforts to use the algorithms of technology platform giants to mislead and confuse people, and a denigration of evidence, expertise, science and empiricism.

Perhaps most menacing, these techniques of denying facts, demonizing the press and the academy, and urging people to believe their leaders rather than mediating institutions, are the proven tools of despots, tyrants and dictators.

The goal of all these is not to persuade the public to believe what is fake. It is to cause people to doubt what is real.

The challenge is that to function properly societies need methods of settling on facts — for juries to come to verdicts, for civic counsels to understand problems and arrive at possible solutions, for people to come together and arrive at compromises.

And the maturity of any society is determined, in part, by its ability to live with doubt and uncertainty and still make progress.

Donald Trump's presidency has created conflicting narratives about the state of journalism. Trump has labeled the press "fake news" and the enemy of the people. At the same time, Trump's assault has stiffened the spine of news organizations covering him, ignited a surge in subscriptions to several national news organizations and spawned unprecedented leaking to the press even within his own West Wing. It is a Dickensian double vision, the best and the worst of times.

It can be difficult, at times, not to worry, as talk show host Charles Sykes wrote breathlessly in America Magazine not long ago:[2]

> *We now find ourselves awash in fabulism, fake news and outright lies, some of them coming from the White House itself. Indeed, even as we wrestle with our political divisions, one of the most consequential questions we now face is whether truth matters anymore. This is no longer a theoretical question for postmodern academics. It is increasingly and existential question for our democracy.*

If we have not quite entered what some call the "post-truth" era, have we entered a period of parallel or competing truths? How did we get here? What does the past offer as a guidepost to where we go next? And to what degree can we say, if people are inclined to ignore them, that facts do matter?

As we search for answers, it is useful to recognize that the battle for truth, and against propaganda and misinformation, is hardly new; nor is it a battle that ever ends.

You will find, in the chapters that follow in this book, counsel about how to practice and identify news that is reliable, as well as why facts and fabulism are at war today and how the public's view of journalists and journalism influences that war.

HOW WE GOT HERE

Trust in the press began to decline long before the internet, the birth of social media or the 2016 election. According to survey data, the beginning of the decline in trust in the news media started in the 1980s. From 1977 to 1997, according to Gallup, the number of Americans who said they had "a great deal or a fair amount of trust and confidence" in the news media dropped 19 percentage points (from 72 percent to 53 percent), a decline of more than a third.[3]

What explains that drop? The first factor is new technology during that period was creating more consumer choice in media. The most important of these technologies was the advent of cable, which expanded the television dial from four channels to 40, and now closer to 400 (before you count YouTube and digital streaming).

The launch of CNN in 1980 marked the start, though few imagined the changes the channel initially derided as Chicken Noodle News would bring. Little remembered now, CNN broke the hegemony that the three networks had over what video their local affiliates could air prior to the network evening newscasts. CNN began a video sharing service; soon, local stations around the country were airing national stories before their parent networks' newscasts. Even before Fox affiliates began airing news an hour before network affiliates' late news, this break in video control amounted to a major revolution in how people began to get national news.

The advent of cable technology, in turn, led the administration of Ronald Reagan to begin to deregulate electronic media. In short order, we saw the end of the Fairness Doctrine (which required broadcasters to offer contrasting viewpoints in coverage of controversial issues) and the Equal Time Rule (which required broadcasters to offer equivalent opportunity for opposing political candidates who requested time). Conservatives had long been suspicious of these rules established in the 1960s, believing a largely Democrat-dominated government used them to suppress conservative ideas.

The deregulations cleared the path for a loosely regulated cable and digital landscape. They also helped seed the ground for the rise of talk radio in the early 1990s, which quickly marketed itself as the conservative alternative to the liberal mainstream media. Liberated by the Reagan administration deregulations, stations could fill their lineup with hours of conservative talk without any regulatory requirement that they offer viewpoints with a different perspective.

For its part, the rise of cable not only expanded the dial on television and paved the way for deregulation, it also propelled the notion of the 24-7 news cycle — constant news all the time — a generation before the public web.

It is hard to overstate the impact of the continuous news cycle on how journalism was practiced. It amounted to a subtle but profound shift in journalism values. As Bill Kovach and Tom Rosenstiel (co-author of this chapter) wrote in the book "Warp Speed," the traditional "journalism of verification," in which newspeople spent hours working on stories for an evening or morning newscast or newspaper or weekly magazine, began to give way to a new "journalism of assertion," in which the raw ingredients of news — the accusation from a press conference, the off-hand remark made during an interview, the official slip of a tongue at the podium — were now passed on to viewers live.

> *"Suddenly everyone could be in the breaking news business, including newspapers."*

In the journalism of assertion, moreover, influence gradually began to shift from news organizations trying to act as gatekeepers over facts and moved toward the sources who could assert what they wanted without journalists having time to check it before passing it along. In the journalism of assertion, and a world of more outlets, sources began to have more influence over the journalists who covered them.

The continuous news cycle also involved another sea change. In the journalism of assertion, the taped, edited TV package — which had been the staple of the nightly newscasts — was largely supplanted by live interviews and panel discussions as the dominant TV format. In studies by the Project for Excellence in Journalism, we found that the vast majority of time on network news programming was made up of edited packages. In cable news, the vast majority of time was live and unedited.

Why does it matter? In a reported package, reporters could double-check their facts, scripts could be carefully crafted and photos could be matched to words. In the live formats, guests could more easily filibuster, spin or pass on false information. It was difficult for a host to catch everything, let alone risk being rude by challenging guests on details. Eventually comedians like Jon Stewart would mock cable hosts for letting guests get away with false statements, followed, before a commercial break, by the host saying, "We'll have to leave it here."

Network news ratings began to fall rapidly. By 2000, at the dawn of the digital era, the three nightly newscasts had lost half their audience.[4] The conventional press, particularly television, responded to the ratings drop brought on by cable with a new era of sensationalism and tabloidization. Terms like infotainment, the argument culture and the Crossfirization of news became part of the vocabulary. And syndicated tabloid programs like "A Current Affair" and "Access Hollywood" began to dot the television schedule.

And all this — deregulation, expanded technology, falling levels of trust, the invention of the 24-hour, seven-day-a-week news cycle, talk radio and the journalism of assertion — occurred before 1997, the first major wave of decline in trust in media. And all before the internet.

Now add the web. In large part, the first decade of internet publishing (2000 to 2010) tended to intensify the effect of the 24-hour news cycle. Suddenly everyone could be in the breaking news business, including newspapers. Publishers of all stripes found themselves contending with the pressures of the journalism of assertion and the perils of publishing first and verifying second.

Other, even more complex, issues followed. The barriers to publishing fell. Newsmakers and political actors could now publish directly. So could community groups and populations that had been ignored or passed over, whether they were ethnic and gender populations or political factions.

The first great cultural battle inside journalism during the digital age — from about 2004 to 2014 — pitted two groups of influential players against each other: digital utopians enthused by the web's promise versus newsroom leaders concerned with quality who feared the impact of the web on journalism values. Utopians tended to foresee an end to the hegemony of the white, older and establishment news oligarchy. Traditionalists feared a vague assembly of amateurs in pajamas, political propagandists and factless opinion mongers.

Neither vision was fully realized. In many ways, the idea of "citizen journalism" gave way instead to social media. And on social platforms, rather than acting like amateur journalists spending their days reporting stories as a kind of hobby, people behave much more like civic consumers — reading things, passing on what they have seen, adding their comments and short opinions.

In effect, people have not become their own reporters. Instead they have, in a very real sense, become their own editors.

We have also learned social media has a kind of bipolar quality. People tend to share what makes them either euphoric or angry. Content that has less of an emotional impact — that is simply informative — tends not to register on Twitter and Facebook.

In short, while visions of the open web originally imagined an information system that dramatically democratized information and gave voice to the voiceless, as with every technology before it, the web developed in ways its inventors did not envision.

The other unexpected effect of the digital revolution had to do with its corporate structure. Rather than a so-called long tail of small publishers reaching a broad range of audiences — a kind of information democracy — the web became a space where a small number of companies would control distribution. The new oligarchy of the web would be smaller, and its corporate reach deeper, than anything that happened with newspapers, radio or television.

And the trend has only intensified with the mobile web. In 2011, at the peak of the desktop era, five companies controlled two-thirds of all ad revenue online (Google, Facebook, Yahoo, AOL and Microsoft). In mobile, as of 2017, just two companies, Facebook and Google, controlled more than 80 percent of all mobile ad revenue on the web.[5]

Some anticipated the problem. In 2011 Eli Pariser, co-founder of Upworthy, coined the term "filter bubble" and worried about Google's personalized search function that ensured no two people's Google searches would offer the same results. He encouraged those running social media platforms to consider "their algorithms prioritize counter-vailing views and news that's important, not just the stuff that's popular or most self-validating."

But those companies were designed to help advertisers target people. The intention was to connect people with what they wanted and validate their interests by allowing them to see things they'd likely purchase or share with their communities.

It was logical that foreign governments and others would try to divine how to reverse engineer and manipulate those algorithms for political gain.

The platforms themselves generally didn't see it coming. "The cyber security people worried about this, but they were largely treated as people who always worried," one former Google executive told us.

The practice of "Red Teaming" systems — a military concept that involves imagining how something could be exploited by evildoers — was not standard at the platform companies. Indeed, when PBS's Hari Sreenivasan asked executives of the major platforms about this recently at a technology conference, he was met largely by silence.

And one part of the role of search and social in the spread of misinfor-mation is a structural problem that the content producers, not the plat-forms, must address. In traditional media, consumers navigate the news by brand. We watch the CBS Evening News, navigate The New York Times website or mobile app, or read the Dallas Morning News in print. Implicit-ly, we convey our trust to that brand.

That is not how we encounter news on social platforms. There, the news is atomized into individual stories, largely separate from brand. We see pictures shared by a friend, mixed in with an article shared by someone else. And the most important cue, as we discovered in experiments at the American Press Institute, is not who produced the news but who shared it.[6]

It's become fashionable to attribute the rise of "fake news" simply to what is now called confirmation bias, or the idea that people only believe what they want to believe and are immune to facts (see Chapter Four). This notion underlies the concept of the so-called "post fact" society, or the troubling notion that facts no longer matter in an age when people can choose their own news. Human nature, the argument implies, is such that people will only choose what they want.

But there is growing evidence that notion of the psychological filter bubble is oversimplified. To begin with, it turns out that people are consuming news in common spaces more than they may recognize.

Perhaps more important, both cyberforensics and human psychology research are beginning to reveal there is more going on than people being naturally immune to inconvenient information.

A growing body of research, particularly into the impact of the state-sponsored campaign to influence the 2016 election, is confirming that bots — fake Twitter and Facebook accounts programmed by machines or managed by humans to look like people who do not really exist — were critical in spreading phony news stories and getting them in front of unsuspecting audiences.[7]

In some cases, the truly fake news was generated by people in the United States who simply wanted to make a little money. But, we are learning, the network of foreign government bots in social media was essential to that content spreading.

"The point of modern propaganda isn't only to misinform or push an agenda. It is to exhaust your critical thinking, to annihilate truth."

A study by researchers at Indiana University in Bloomington is just one piece of the broadening network of evidence.[8] The team monitored 400,000 claims by sites known to create fake news, collected across some 14 million Twitter posts. The researchers found that bots were far more likely to be the active Twitter accounts spreading misinformation. What's more, the bots were far more likely to target so-called network influencers — that is, people or accounts that are actively followed by more people. Indeed, the foreign schemes to spread fake news, network cybersecurity experts say, are built around identifying powerful social influencers, linking to them and then getting them to unwittingly spread false information to their networks.

The point of fake news is also more subtle than some may realize. The goal of fake news is not to persuade people to believe the false information. It is to get them to doubt real news, or to become so exhausted by the effort of deciphering real news amid the fake reports that they give up and retreat to their preconceptions.

Former chess grandmaster and now Russian dissident Garry Kasparov, who has battled with Russian President Vladimir Putin's government, has written: "The point of modern propaganda isn't only to misinform or push an agenda. It is to exhaust your critical thinking, to annihilate truth."[9]

Science backs up the theory.

The "illusory truth effect" is a term used by scholars to describe a thinking shortcut that helps our brains retain information. The basic idea is the more we hear about something, the more likely we are to remember it. It's usually studied in an experiment that asks participants to rate trivial statements as true or false. Days, weeks and sometimes even months later, the experimenters bring the participants back to test. The second time, some of the statements appeared in the original study and some are new.

Research in psychology finds that the more often we hear, or see, or consume information, the more likely we are to believe it.[10] Psychologist Gord Pennycook at Yale University notes that after repeated exposure to incorrect information people will even begin to believe things they know not to believe.

In 2015, Lisa Fazio, a psychologist at Vanderbilt University, found even previous knowledge about the subject doesn't stop the illusory truth effect. Fazio's study engaged people who knew Scottish men wear kilts. Yet even those people could be persuaded to doubt the fact if they were repeatedly exposed to the idea that Scottish men wear saris. Repetition of the falsehood made the statement appear more and more plausible each time it was read.

There is something positive to be found in this research as well. The problem is not that people are immune to facts or so captive to their own biases that they are unable to know what's true. No one has a confirmation bias to wish that Scottish men wear Saris. We are not, in other words, hopelessly doomed by confirmation bias. And it required an organized state-sponsored campaign to create the repetition to make fake news work in the 2016 election, a problem that in theory at least can be addressed.

So if people can come to facts, how can news organizations and others help make that happen?

WHAT JOURNALISTS CAN DO

In the last few years, well before the 2016 election, a host of efforts were underway to try to rebuild trust with news.

For many, the concept of being more transparent with audiences about methods, practices and the philosophy of newsgathering is at the heart of trying to rebuild. For others, listening to their audience, asking what questions they want answered, and turning news into more of a conversation and less of a lecture are at the core of rebuilding trust.

The Trust Project at the University of Santa Clara has used scholarly methods to identify "trust indicators" that provide clarity on not only the organization, but journalists' backgrounds and how their work came to be.

Joy Mayer at the Reynolds Journalism Institute's Trusting News project[11] has worked with 28 newsrooms to identify other approaches to transparency, including the finding that people unfamiliar with journalists or news organizations are less inclined to trust them. These projects aim to change that perception.

Other efforts, such as The Coral Project, Listening Post and a company called Hearken, are working on ways in which journalists and news organizations can more effectively listen to their audiences, turning news into more of a conversation, creating news that answers questions from the community and covering issues in ways that are more relevant and useful. Solutions Journalism, in turn, is an organization that works to make news coverage more comprehensive and useful by ensuring that it includes solutions being discussed around issues, moving beyond the old journalistic reflex to primarily spotlight problems and leave it at that.

THE ROLE OF PLATFORM COMPANIES IN THE PROBLEM

One major question, of course, involves what the platform companies, particularly Google, Facebook and Twitter, will do to filter out news that has been proven false or that was fabricated deliberately to mislead or confuse.

It can be at times difficult to answer that question. The platform companies themselves do not tend to be all that transparent about their algorithms and systems.

As the year 2017 wore on, the efforts by Facebook, Twitter and others to assure consumers they were trying to address the problems were confounded by

> *"Facebook and Google are opaque. Their algorithms are black boxes. Their strategies are secret."*

more information on just how susceptible their platforms were to being manipulated by organized foreign campaigns to spread false information and influence American elections.

By October 2017, Facebook began labeling news stories with "Disputed by 3rd party fact-checkers" and saw impressions on those misleading sites drop by 80 percent. But the labeling process takes up to three days, and in the case of breaking news, the initial impressions matter the most.

The research, moreover, on fact-checking itself is mixed. Research has found that no one likes the candidates they support to be fact-checked.[12] Republicans are more skeptical of the practice than Democrats. And while fact-checking can be effective in some cases, there is also evidence of what some call a "backfire" effect. Roddy Roediger, an expert on learning and memory at Washington University in Saint Louis, puts it this way: "When you see a news report that repeats the misinformation and then tries to correct it, you might have people remembering the misinformation because it's really surprising and interesting, and not remembering the correction."

Tom Williams/CQ Roll Call

Facebook CEO Mark Zuckerberg prepares to testify before the House Energy and Commerce Committee on the protection of user data on April 11, 2018.

In the case of Facebook, there may be a more fundamental issue at play. The platform continuously says it is not a content provider and thus will not block speech. Usually Facebook executives describe this as a philosophical commitment to an open web and free speech, embedded in the values and DNA of the company in its quest to make the world better through open connections.

However, some believe this argument is now as much a legal defense by a large, rich corporation as it is a matter of philosophy. If Facebook were to begin to make editorial decisions about the propriety of user content rather than advertising, some lawyers argue, it could be liable for any content on the site, inviting massive litigation that could hobble the company.

Some journalists have tried to read the tea leaves of Mark Zuckerberg's occasional essays as well as occasional white papers the company makes public.[13] For the most part, however, Facebook and Google are opaque. Their algorithms are black boxes. Their strategies are secret. Visitors sign non-disclosure statements to walk on their properties. Any notions of transparency, integral to the journalistic ethos, are largely anathema in the secretive, vertically integrated and monopolistic world of Silicon Valley.

By and large, Facebook's efforts to say it is trying to fix problems and help journalism were met with growing skepticism as 2017 moved into 2018. In Washington, where legislators in both parties are increasingly angry with the platforms, Facebook has far more problems nine months after the election than it did the day after. Its efforts at putting the election behind it, as 2017 came to close, appeared largely ineffective.

One reason is that influential writers, some of whom were enthusiastic about the platforms, have become skeptical about the technology companies in the same way that doubters have always been.

In October, when a gunman killed more than 50 people in Las Vegas, both the Atlantic and The New York Times noted that the rapid elevation of misinformation on Facebook and Google suggested their efforts to correct the problems nearly a year after the 2016 election had made little progress. Google's algorithms reached out to less authoritative figures in order to show something, anything, which rapidly spread across social media in the aftermath of the shooting.

The New York Times has criticized the automation of editorial judgment that tech companies reiterated following the shooting, declaring it a "lopsided battle between those who want to spread misinformation and those tasked with policing it."

Not long after, the Atlantic's influential technology writer Alexis Madrigal authored a cover story suggesting that while many technology reporters knew some things were happening at Facebook, it took the results of the 2016 election and the ensuing fallout to make them realize "no one knew everything that was going on at Facebook, not even Facebook."

WHY TRUTH MATTERS

Where does that leave journalism and its embedded value in pursuing facts and truth?

In my book with Bill Kovach, "The Elements of Journalism," we say that "journalism's first obligation is to the truth." It was the one value on which research on those who practiced journalism all agreed. And by truth we meant more than accuracy.

In 1947, the Hutchins Commission on Freedom of the Press was thinking about the meaning of accuracy and truth as its members pondered the implications of the arrival of radio and television. The commission concluded that it is not enough to publish accounts of events that are "factually correct but substantially untrue." Context matters. Stereotypes, lack of context, false inference, cherry-picked information — any of those can make accurate facts false. The commission declared: "It is no longer enough to report the truthfully. It is now necessary to report the truth about the fact."[14]

> *"Journalism's first obligation is to the truth."*

Today we live in an age when even images can be falsified by algorithmic technology.

The ease of falsifying information, however, makes the need for truth greater, not lesser. The challenge is also not new. The quote has been attributed to many before this, but assign it to Winston Churchill if you will, who was among those who said in the mid-20th century that "a lie can move around the world while the truth is still putting its pants on."

Writing after the election of 2016, Yale historian Timothy Snyder in his book "On Tyranny" declared, "Believe in truth. To abandon facts is to abandon freedom."

We hope this book provokes thoughts for those invested in society operating on a foundation of facts. In its chapters, there is advice for news consumers, as well as those producing the news, on things they can do to better separate deliberately fake news, propaganda and rumors from reliable information.

Sen. Moynihan was not entirely right when he said people are not entitled to their own facts. Facts, by their nature, require being put in order until they reveal something true. But he was right about one thing even more fundamental. We need facts. And we need truth.

CHAPTER TWO

Finding Our Way

By Frank Sesno

Finding Our Way

Joshua Hatch knows what he's doing around journalism and the disrupted world of data and social media. President of the Online News Association in 2017, Hatch has provided multimedia training for journalists all over the world. And as the assistant managing editor of data and interactives at the Chronicle of Higher Education, Hatch inspires data reporters, designers and developers to tell stories in creative, effective and digital ways. Yet some of Hatch's most compelling observations about media come from his experience as the father of a 14-year-old daughter. Her world has always been one of nonstop content, media from all sides, at all times of the day and night, flying "fast and furious." Hatch is concerned, as any father should be, about whether his daughter can distinguish digital dangers from credible content that can inform and enlighten. It's not easy.

"She doesn't want me to sit down and give her a news literacy lecture," Hatch told me. But he wants his daughter to know how to tell good from bad, true from false, fact from opinion. So he talks to her about knowing the sources of news and recognizable brands. He tells his daughter that if she sees a story on Facebook, "don't just read the story, but click in and do your due diligence about where the story actually came from." He talks about stories that revel in sensationalism and hyperbole, explaining, "If it really seems astounding and amazing, that's a signal that you need to look at it a little bit more." Hatch is guardedly optimistic that his daughter has a realistic approach to her news consumption, guided by a healthy skepticism and the right questions to determine if information is trustworthy.

But for those who haven't been inoculated against the epidemic of deliberately false news stories and manipulative social media content, Hatch wonders if perhaps we just haven't "built up our fake news antibodies yet."

Joshua Hatch

"Don't just read the story, but click in and do your due diligence about where the story actually came from."

Citizens and news consumers have work to do if they're going to build stronger immune systems. They will need to be more informed and engaged with the news. They will need to recognize that content comes from a vast array of sources and platforms: traditional and nontraditional reporters; advocates and activists; talk show hosts and opinionated experts or pseudo-experts; bots; conspiracy theorists; provocateurs intending to misinform for kicks or for malign intent; and hostile governments, who want to deliberately distort and misinform in order to sow confusion and discord.

How can consumers, many already deeply distrustful of the media, navigate? How can they identify quality journalism and distinguish well-sourced credible information from fictitious, unsubstantiated or malevolent information? What should readers, viewers and listeners look for as they try to be more informed and trusting consumers of news? It starts with an awareness of the stakes and dimensions of the problem.

THE PROBLEM

Hoaxes and fabricated news have been around for a long time. By today's standards, the National Enquirer's fictitious fare seems almost quaint: alien abductions and drunk dogs alongside more salacious "reporting" alleging that a prostitute murdered Supreme Court Justice Antonin Scalia, that Brad Pitt had it in for Angelina Jolie, or that Sen. Ted Cruz was fooling around with multiple women. Intrigue sells. Conspiracy theories have drawn audiences throughout history. You've probably heard: FDR secretly knew Japan was going to attack Pearl Harbor; Lyndon Johnson was involved in the assassination of John F. Kennedy; the U.S. government had a hand in the 9/11 attacks. Americans have lots of experience in the unsubstantiated and the unproven built on fabricated, exaggerated or presumed facts.

But today, with the amplification and audiences of social media, and with content delivered to our digital doorsteps often without any filtering, false information can gain an unprecedented foothold. A blogger in Macedonia, a mischief-maker in Moscow, a headline-grabber in Buffalo can fabricate a story, make a video or share a phony "article" that looks exactly like one from an established website or news organization. Against this backdrop, news consumers must be newly vigilant and constantly aware. They must be able to distinguish fact from opinion, understand what constitutes credible journalism and know how to spot blatantly false or unreliable news, no matter where it comes from.

Some stories are disseminated across social media with no checking and are flat-out wrong.[1] The online forum 4chan featured message boards that incorrectly identified the Las Vegas shooter who killed more than 50 people in Las Vegas on Oct. 1, 2017. The false claim led to a story on Gateway Pundit headlined, "Las Vegas Shooter Reportedly a Democrat Who Liked Rachel Maddow, MoveOn.org and Associated with Anti-Trump Army." This played to a deeply divisive narrative, suggesting that the massacre was politically motivated.

Other stories are intended to parody the news or drive revenue-generating traffic through social media shares. A story saying that rat meat was

Jose Luis Magana/AP

The front door of Comet Ping Pong pizza shop in Washington, D.C. Edgar Maddison Welch of Salisbury, N.C., who police said was inspired by false internet rumors, fired an assault-style weapon inside a Washington pizzeria.

being sold as chicken wings to satisfy Super Bowl appetites earned a Facebook warning,[2] but the company reported that the post had been shared more than 175,000 times.

False stories can be propelled by a highly charged narrative — incredible stories that reinforce strongly held emotions, fears or beliefs. On Nov. 16, 2016, a headline on Omnithought.org screamed, "Pizzagate: How 4Chan Uncovered the Sick World of Washington's Occult Elite." The infamous "Pizzagate" story ricocheted through social media. It alleged that Democratic presidential nominee Hillary Clinton and her former campaign chairman John Podesta were running a child sex ring from the basement of a Washington, D.C., pizzeria, Comet Ping Pong. There was no basement and no sex ring. But Edgar Welch, having read the stories online, decided that he should investigate the problem himself. He drove 350 miles from his home in North Carolina to Washington, walked into Comet Ping Pong on Sunday, Dec. 4, 2016, and fired an assault rifle. Fortunately, no one was hurt. But false news could have had fatal results.

Far less dangerous, but just as challenging for news consumers, is partisan content that is funded by advocates, activists and think tanks but designed to look and sound like independent news reporting. Using the language, titles and look of traditional news, it can add to consumer confusion. From the right, the Daily Signal, a product of the conservative Heritage Foundation, says it "delivers investigative and feature reporting and the most important political news and commentary." The editorial team, readers are told, "is committed to truth and unmatched in knowledge of Washington's politics and policy debates." Stories promote conservative causes: "Former White House Insider Explains What Trump Did to Devastate ISIS" or "Pro-Life Students Sue Miami University Because It Won't Let Them Erect A Cross." The Daily Signal's editor-in-chief, Robert Bluey, is qualified but hardly dispassionate, having cut his teeth at a string of outspokenly conservative media outlets including the Daily Caller, RedState, Big Government and the Washington Examiner.

On the other side of the political divide, ThinkProgress is the content producer for the liberal Center for American Progress. It offers "reporting" with a decidedly left-leaning activist approach. Judd Legum is editor-in-chief. He started ThinkProgress in 2005, left to work as research director for Hillary Clinton's 2008 presidential campaign, then returned to ThinkProgress and became its editor-in-chief. On its About page, ThinkProgress boasts a "newsroom of reporters and editors covering the intersections between politics, policy, culture and social justice." But you have to look past the word "news" to discern the organization's true mission: "ThinkProgress is a news site dedicated to providing our readers with rigorous reporting and analysis from a progressive perspective." ThinkProgress stories come in from the hard left: "Here's What's at Stake for the 21 Kids Suing the Trump Administration Over Climate Change" or "Minnesota Lawmaker Mocks Students Who Asked for Meeting, Says She Won't Meet With Democrats."

None of this compares to the egregious assault of phony, false and hateful stories blasted in from beyond America's borders during the 2016 U.S. presidential campaign.

Russia's exact efforts remain unclear at the time of this writing. But U.S. intelligence agencies and researchers who have dug into the problem concluded the evidence points to an alarming and pervasive campaign of misinformation, false news and insidious propaganda dressed up to look legitimate and even familiar. Russian operatives bought some 3,000 ads on Facebook, posted videos and stories, created memes, and used bogus identities. Jonathan Albright, research director of the Tow Center for Digital Journalism at Columbia University, researched Russia's interference in the 2016 U.S. presidential election. He estimates that Russian-controlled Facebook pages and accounts had been shared hundreds of millions of times. Albright also found Russian disinformation on Twitter, YouTube, Instagram, Pinterest and Google. He describes the Russian effort as "cultural hacking" and told The New York Times, "They are using systems that were already set up by these platforms to increase engagement. They're feeding outrage — and it's easy to do because outrage and emotion is how people share."[3]

Outrage and emotion have been persistent, corrosive elements in the assault on media and have contributed to the crisis of confidence in truth-seeking journalism. From Rush Limbaugh to Fox News, Matt Drudge to Breitbart, much of conservative media have thrived on attacking "mainstream" (which they consider liberal) media. They criticize not just the quality of the coverage but the motivations behind it, suggesting that the media are part of some grand conspiracy or an extension of the "deep state."

> *"They're feeding outrage — and it's easy to do because outrage and emotion is how people share."*

It's been argued that the left-leaning positions of the editorial pages of The New York Times and The Washington Post have bled into their news pages, or that CNN's harshly critical coverage of President Donald Trump has become a knee-jerk obsession that has tainted its self-proclaimed status as the "most trusted name in news." But the suggestion that these news organizations constitute the opposition, even the "enemy of the American people" as the president tweeted in his first month in office, has taken the attacks to a dangerous new level and further polarized the public's attitudes toward media. A December 2017 YouGov poll found that 60 percent of Trump supporters agreed with his characterization of the media as an "enemy."[4] One in four Americans said they support limitations on press freedom. Those hardening attitudes were in stark contrast to increased confidence in the press among self-identified Democrats. Nearly three-quarters, 74 percent, of Democrats expressed a "great deal" or "fair amount" of confidence.

Efforts to undermine fact-based reporting and journalistic reputation took a bizarre turn in November 2017, when The Washington Post discovered a deliberate effort to entrap its reporters. A woman who identified herself as Jaime T. Phillips approached the Post with the sensational claim that Republican Alabama Senate candidate Roy Moore had gotten her pregnant when she was 15 years old. Moore was already under a cloud for alleged sexual advances toward teenage girls when he was in his thirties. Phillips wanted an assurance that her story would destroy Moore. In effect, she wanted the Post reporter to take sides. Phillips was a plant, secretly recording her conversations with Post reporters while working for Project Veritas activist James O'Keefe, who had used hidden cameras and dubious editing to embarrass organizations such as Planned Parenthood and NPR in the past. Asked about the ruse, O'Keefe told an audience not long after, "Yes, we use disguise, yes, we go undercover, but sometimes it's the only way to ferret out what people really believe." He defended his rule-breaking approach. "At Veritas, we believe that we're all journalists now."

SOCIAL MEDIA AS THE GREAT AMPLIFIER

Of course, we're not all journalists now. As we've seen, not everyone plays by the rules commonly recognized as the pillars of journalistic professionalism: accuracy, a discipline of verification, pursuit of truth, and accountability if you get it wrong. Holding a pen, having an opinion, recording a conversation or pointing a camera — concealed or otherwise — does not convey journalist status any more than removing a splinter lets you claim to be a doctor, or cooking a meal confers status as a chef.

But social media and digital dissemination convey informational power to the individual that is unprecedented in human history. Anyone can post a story. Friends and followers can create instant networks. A single video can generate millions of views. Facebook is a bigger network with a more extensive reach than any network on the planet. By the end of 2017, the company reported that 1.3 billion people were active on the platform every day, 2.1 billion every month. Facebook says its mission "is to give people the power to build community and bring the world closer together." But Facebook's own experience with bots and bad actors, Russia and the 2016 U.S. presidential election shows what it — and every news consumer — is up against.

In September 2017, Facebook Chief Security Officer Alex Stamos posted disturbing information the company had uncovered about Russian activities during the 2016 election campaign that pointed to a stunning level of precision and subterfuge in how the Russian operatives worked. While most of their content didn't directly reference the campaign or candidates, he wrote, "the ads and accounts appeared to focus on amplifying divisive social and political messages across the ideological spectrum — touching on topics from LGBT matters to race issues to immigration to gun rights." Many were aimed squarely at communities where divisions and tensions already simmered.

Ben Nimmo, information defense fellow with the Atlantic Council's Digital Forensic Research Lab, has been studying disinformation in the media for nearly 20 years. He is most concerned about the kind of fake news "that plants false information and evil intent" at the same time. He calls it "hyper-emotional interpretation." Nimmo points out that social media trolls in St. Petersburg, Russia, triggered a confrontation between pro-Muslim and anti-Islam demonstrators in Texas in May 2016. The standoff ended without bloodshed, but showed Russia's ability to weaponize the anger of American citizens thousands of miles away. "It's what Russian military calls the 'protest potential of the population,'" Nimmo explains. He points to paragraph 15a of Russia's 2014 military doctrine, which notes that characteristics of military conflicts include "informational or other non-military measures implemented with a wide use of the protest potential of the population and special operations forces."

Nimmo cites another example, not from a foreign government but from a major British tabloid. A Daily Mail story following the United Kingdom's vote to leave the European Union headlined a ruling by a panel of judges that Brexit could not be initiated without a vote first from parliament. To some, it seemed the judges were intervening, playing politics. The Daily Mail's headline fairly shouted from the page: "Enemies of the people: Fury over 'out of touch' judges who have 'declared war on democracy' by defying 17.4m Brexit voters and who could trigger constitutional crisis." Nimmo explains that it was the angry, fear-inducing characterization of the story — built upon real facts — that made

> *"If you want to manipulate people, you make them angry and you make them afraid."*

it so effective and so poisonous. He believes informed news consumers will have to learn to spot and navigate around this kind of coverage — from familiar and unfamiliar news sources alike. "If you want to manipulate people, you make them angry and you make them afraid."

Perhaps, then, when a reader encounters the Sputnik news site, which bills itself as "a modern news agency whose products include newsfeeds, websites, social networks, mobile apps, radio broadcasts and multimedia press centers," he or she will know that a story like "Hillary, Queen of War: The Road Map Ahead"[3] is going for the gut, not the brain. A Google search brings up the Wikipedia entry on Sputniknews.com, which states that Sputnik is an arm of the Russian government.

REGAINING TRUST

Against this backdrop of pernicious information from so many different sources, it is hardly surprising that Americans have become suspicious of the information they consume. A 2017 Gallup survey on "confidence in institutions" found that only about a quarter of Americans have a "great deal" or "quite a lot" of confidence in newspapers or television news. A

Pew Research Center survey taken shortly after the 2016 presidential election found that 64 percent of American adults felt "fabricated news stories cause a great deal of confusion about the basic facts of current issues and events." Nearly a third said they "often" see made-up political news online. A scant 5 percent of adults who get news from social media have a lot of trust in the information they see there.[6]

The University of Missouri's Trusting News project conducted a study in 2017 across 28 newsrooms asking 8,728 people about their attitudes toward media and the news sources they trusted most and least.[7] The list is instructive. The Economist, public television, Reuters, the BBC, NPR, the Guardian and the Wall Street Journal topped the list for trustworthy news. Least trusted were BuzzFeed, Breitbart and social media generally.[8]

Media watchdogs, political leaders and the public have called for social media giants to recognize their responsibilities and crack down on the flow of blatantly false news. In April 2017, Facebook's vice president for News Feed, Adam Mosseri, acknowledged the challenge: "We know people want to see accurate information on Facebook — and so do we. False news is harmful to our community, it makes the world less informed, and it erodes trust."[9]

Facebook launched a multipronged effort: "disrupt" the economic incentives behind misleading information, come up with new tools to "curb the spread of false news" and help people "make more informed decisions when they encounter false news." Facebook is placing its biggest bet on its community of readers and viewers to be more aware and engaged, and to thread their own needles of fact and fiction.

Facebook now asks members to flag suspicious content so the company can turn it over to outside fact-checkers. If these independent third parties find dubious claims, fabricated quotes or other problems, Facebook will indicate the item contains disputed content. The company has even produced a video explaining how this works. A reader will see a headline stating "Disputed by 3rd parties" followed by an advisory: "Before you share this story, you might want to know that independent fact-checkers disputed its accuracy." You're then free to click "Cancel" or "Continue."

KNOWING NEWS

If readers, viewers and listeners are to be the vanguard of quality, fact-based journalism, what steps can they take to, as Joshua Hatch described it, build up their fake news antibodies? How can they distinguish legitimate news from deliberately fictitious or misleading news? How can citizens contribute to an information environment less polluted by foul runoff from troll factories and bots? What should news consumers look for? What should they find conspicuous by its absence?

First, consumers should understand the basic ingredients of accurate, evidence-based reporting, and news organizations should help with this in clear, accessible and consistent ways.

Responsible reporting, whether from news organizations whose editorial pages lean left or right, includes several basic but non-negotiable ingredients: a dedication

"There's too much sensationalism, misinformation and polarization in the world today."

to truth and accuracy; a culture of verification and multiple sourcing; editorial vetting, checking and challenge; a commitment to represent differing points of view; procedures to acknowledge and correct errors; and a code of conduct to guide journalists' behavior and assert accountability. These ingredients should be clearly labeled and publicly accessible. The Wall Street Journal, NPR, the Associated Press, ProPublica and The New York Times post their ethics and news practices online. Consumers should use them to understand the standards, practices and values that govern news organizations they frequent.

Look for a coherent policy on sourcing. The Washington Post's Policies and Standards spell out the approach in considerable detail. "We must be truthful about the source of our information. Facts and quotations in a story that were not produced by our own reporting must be attributed. Attribution of material from other media must be total. Plagiarism is not permitted." The Post goes so far as to explain the difference between "on the record," "background," "deep background" and "off the record" sourcing. Its bottom-line goal is "clarity in our dealings with sources and readers. This means explaining our ground rules to sources, and giving readers as much information as possible about how we learned the information in our stories."

The best sourcing involves multiple, named, knowledgeable sources with direct access to issues and information relevant to the story. The sources' backgrounds and agendas should be plainly stated and it should be clear if they are decision-makers, partisans, loyalists, adversaries, experts or eyewitnesses.

When it comes to unnamed sources, news consumers should look for an explanation as to why the sources are anonymous and their proximity to the story. Many news organizations have decided to use fewer anonymous sources and to provide as much background as possible when they are essential to the story, indicating the source's agenda, degree of direct knowledge, professional background or ideological persuasion.

How to spot a suspect or bogus unnamed source? Look for unsubstantiated claims, highly emotional appeals or accusations, name-calling or demonizing. Be wary of anonymous sources who allege cover-ups and conspiracy theories without producing any evidence or who appear in a story that lacks corroboration from other interviews, on-the-record statements, photos, emails or documents.

Also, look for a description of a news organization's process for assessing anonymous sources and determining whether the information they possess reaches a threshold where anonymity is warranted. The investigative ProPublica news site provides explicit guidance on its Code of Ethics page. "Editors have an obligation to know the identity of unnamed sources in our stories, so that editors and reporters can jointly assess the appropriateness of using their information. Sources need to understand this practice." ProPublica's commitment to transparency is exemplary. Its clarity and detail provide a roadmap for consumers and should set the standard for the industry.

"We don't misidentify or misrepresent ourselves to get a story. When we seek an interview, we identify ourselves as ProPublica journalists," the code states. "We don't pay for interviews. We don't plagiarize. Nothing in our work should be fabricated. We don't use pseudonyms, composite characters or fictional names, ages, places or dates."

Still, no matter how informed the reader or how much trust a news organization engenders, there will be bad days. Very bad days. Mistakes and bad reporting are journalists' worst nightmares. They misinform the audience, damage credibility and erode trust. But they happen. Some will be innocent and minor: a reporter transposes a number, confuses a timeline of events or applies a statistic incorrectly. Some errors, however, are egregious: an unethical reporter makes up a quote or a reporting team overlooks evidence or leaps to conclusions to allege wrongdoing.

Trustworthy news organizations have systems in place to correct errors and hold themselves and their reporters accountable. ProPublica explains to readers, "Any time a question of fairness or accuracy is raised about any aspect of our work, whether by a source, subject or member of the public, the reporters involved should discuss the issue with their supervising editor and decide what response is warranted. When mistakes are made, they need to be corrected — fully, quickly and ungrudgingly." News organizations should explain their corrections policies within their standards and practices guidelines.

"We must be truthful about the source of our information."

A MATTER OF OPINION

Next, consumers must recognize the distinction between news and opinion. Amid the glut of online news, analysis, commentary, snapchats and tweets competing with the talk-soaked world of cable television, radio and podcast, there may be no line that has become more blurred. In an environment where political agendas often drive coverage, many consumers may view all news as opinionated, biased and motivated by ideology or an agenda. When political commentators and partisan "analysts" mix it up with reporters on TV, the distinctions become positively confounding.

Serious news organizations — whatever their medium — should clearly and prominently label their coverage, asking themselves serious questions about placement, purpose and optics. On a mobile device, do opinion pieces intermingle with reported news stories? Can an untrained reader tell the difference? On television, is a news reporter sitting next to a commentator where, even if everyone is clearly identified, the reporter looks like just another opinionated panelist? In the endless and extemporaneous world of talk, are reporters engaging in debate, appearing to take a position?

To navigate the news-versus-opinion battlefield, consumers must have their radar on at all times. Responsible news organizations should help guide them by properly identifying stories, interviews and content for what they are. The Washington Post has tried to

> *"We don't misidentify or misrepresent ourselves to get a story."*

do this with tags that it puts on stories and columns that reflect opinion or analysis. Post media columnist Margaret Sullivan told me that when she started her job in 2016, she got criticism because her columns reflected a point of view. "I would often hear from readers by email or social media saying in essence, 'It's terrible that your articles include your opinion.'" She wrote back to explain that columnists were supposed to express opinion. Then the Post started putting the tag "Perspective" at the top of the column. Online readers who hover over the word will see just what the Post means and what Sullivan does: "Discussion of news topics with a point of view, including narratives by individuals regarding their own experiences." Sullivan says it made a difference. "Once the tags went on the story, that kind of complaining I got early on essentially disappeared. So, I think it works."

The point here is that consumers can use a variety of tools to become more news literate and more discerning. And journalism organizations should commit themselves to offering those tools to explain what they do, how they do it, what goes into it and what perspective it represents.

A CHECKLIST FOR NEWS

Consumers can develop a "news checklist" to spot bogus news and slow its spread.

· **Don't share**, "like," retweet or otherwise promote through your own social media a news story unless you know and trust its source.

· **If you don't know the site or organization,** do a search. See if it's a partisan player or of suspicious origin. Check out the web address, looking for unusual numbers, dashes or abbreviations of foreign countries. Some bogus sites use legitimate-sounding names such as "The Boston Tribune." Click on "About Us" and see if there is a description of the organization. Look for names and profiles of executives, reporters, senior editors and producers. Click on "Contact Us" and see if there actually are contacts, numbers and addresses at the organization or just fields to put in the reader's name and email. See who the funders or advertisers are.

· **Use fact-checkers** such as Snopes, PolitiFact and Factcheck.org to see if the organization or site has been called out for inaccurate reporting or bad stories in the past.

· **Look at the particulars of a story.** Is there a date, a byline and a dateline? These are basic indicators of legitimate news stories. From the byline, can you click through and see a bio of the reporter? Does he or she have a track record of work? Within the story, are there hyperlinks to other sources, documents or articles, clips or quotes that add information and support the reporting? Does the story feature any opposing voices? Is there a "reality check" of healthy skepticism or does it parrot a particular point of view throughout? Are sources named or unnamed? If they're named, have you heard of them? Are their backgrounds and organizations clearly identified? If the sources are unnamed, especially if they're alleging wrongdoing or stoking fear or emotion, does the reporter explain why and provide context?

· **Pay attention to the ads.** If the story is populated by a lot of pop-up ads or ads that feature sensational headlines or sexual innuendo, the content may be little more than revenue-generating clickbait.

· **Read laterally.** Stanford University researchers Sam Wineburg and Sarah McGrew urge news consumers to follow the example of professional fact-checkers. Open a series of tabs as you go, googling other stories, sites and references. Click on links or footnotes to check sources. Having observed fact-checkers, Wineburg and McGrew write, "Lateral reading contrasts with vertical reading. Reading vertically, our eyes go up and down a screen to evaluate the features of a site. Does it look professional, free of typos and banner ads? Does it quote well-known sources? Are bias or faulty logic detectable? In contrast, lateral readers paid little attention to such features, leaping off a site after a few seconds and opening new tabs. They investigated a site by leaving it."[10]

All of this represents a lot of work for news consumers, who once just opened their newspaper or watched the evening news and considered the source familiar and, to a remarkable degree, trustworthy. No more. Increasingly, citizens who care about the quality of the information they consume, and who want to promote a society where opinions and decisions are based on fact and truth, must be proactive and engaged.

Stanford and New York University researchers Hunt Allcott and Matthew Gentzkow examined the relationship of social media and "fake news" in the 2016 election. They found unprecedented impact: "Content can be relayed among users with no significant third-party filtering, fact-checking or editorial judgment. An individual user with no track record or reputation can in some cases reach as many readers as Fox News, CNN or The New York Times."[11]

Allcott and Gentzkow identified four distinct effects that false, misleading or deliberately fictitious news has on political discourse and governance.

> **First,** "consumers who mistake a fake outlet for a legitimate one have less-accurate beliefs."

> **Second,** because less-accurate beliefs affect decision-making, false news may hurt democracy by "undermining the ability of the democratic process to select high-quality candidates."

> **Third,** the proliferation of false news may also drive consumers to "become more skeptical of legitimate news producers, to the extent that they become hard to distinguish from fake news producers."

> **Finally,** "a reduced demand for high-precision, low-bias reporting will reduce the incentives to invest in accurate reporting." After all, if opinion and debate shows drive ratings and profits, why bother producing a news show that will require more time and effort and be less lucrative?

In a hopeful sign, we see strong signals from a number of "high-precision" news organizations and consumers alike indicating that there remains a significant appetite for quality news. Despite attacks on the free press in the United States and elsewhere, subscriptions and ratings have soared at many news organizations defined by deep reporting, guided by established journalistic practices and principles, committed to breaking news and holding the powerful to account. The business model may not have kept up with the digital transition, but public appetite appears healthy. We remain hunters and gatherers of information.

Fake news has been around as long as people have had something to suspect, say or sell. Governments have engaged in spin and propaganda through the ages. Conspiracy theories have proved contagious. In our social-media, always-on digital world, however, the amount and the velocity of fabricated news are unprecedented. The epidemic is real. The consequences can cause serious damage. News organizations must work harder to deliver quality work and explain themselves. But it falls to each citizen, each news consumer, to take the steps necessary to develop "fake-news antibodies." Otherwise, the society that Joshua Hatch's daughter and every other 14-year-old inherits could be one that cannot tell fact from fiction, news from opinion, democracy from autocracy.

Rachel Reh, a graduate student at The George Washington University School of Media and Public Affairs, contributed to this chapter.

CHAPTER THREE

The Weaponizing Of Fake News

By Bryan Monroe

The Weaponizing
Of Fake News

Wielded by emperors, deployed by chancellors and brandished by presidents, disinformation — or fake news — has been an effective political weapon of dictatorships, as well as democracies, for centuries.

In 44 B.C., following the assassination of Julius Caesar[1] (his friend Brutus and a group of conspirators stabbed him 23 times on the Senate floor), a struggle for power broke out between respected general Marc Antony and Octavian, the adopted son of the slain leader.

So Octavian turned to fake news. He spread rumors that Antony was a sex addict and a ruined soldier, and had been having an illicit romance with Cleopatra, the head of Roman rival Egypt. He even printed snappy catchphrases on coins — the tweets of the time — to spread the word. It worked. In 31 B.C., Octavian won, changed his name to Augustus, and was proclaimed the first emperor of Rome.

Centuries later, Reich Minister of Propaganda for Nazi Germany Joseph Goebbels mastered the use of fake news. Among his tenets, according to "Goebbels' Principles of Propaganda" by Leonard W. Doob,[2] Goebbels believed that "propaganda must label events and people with distinctive phrases or slogans." The phrases must be "easily learned," "evoke desired responses" and "be boomerang-proof." Finally, Goebbels understood that "propaganda must facilitate the displacement of aggression by specifying the targets for hatred."

In the United States in 2016, that target was the media.

Throughout the presidential campaign, the label of "fake news" was frequently deployed, both as an accurate description of content that had been entirely invented — often by Russian-sponsored sites abroad — and as a political bullet to discredit real, factual stories that ran afoul of a particular ideology, opinion or personality.

More often than not, that personality belonged to Donald Trump, the 45th president of the United States.

Trump often wields his favorite sword — his more than 51 million followers on Twitter — to chop down legitimate news stories and target journalists who report facts he does not like. Since his inauguration, Trump has tweeted more than 3,000 times. In many of those tweets — as well as in speeches, interviews and news conferences — he has used the phrase "fake news" hundreds, if not thousands, of times, including at least 150 times on Twitter alone (on one day in September 2017, he said it eight times).[3] And often, he makes it personal.

Just ask CNN's Jim Acosta.

On Aug. 14, 2017, as temperatures in the nation's capital reached 81 degrees with a sweltering 78 percent humidity, the White House press corps gathered in the Diplomatic Reception Room to cover Trump's announcement of an investigation into China's intellectual property laws.[4]

Two days earlier, violence erupted in Charlottesville, Virginia, when white nationalists clashed with anti-fascist protesters in one of the deadliest confrontations over race and neo-Nazism in recent U.S. history. One woman was killed when a car driven by a white nationalist plowed through a crowd of protesters.

The president had been widely criticized for his initial reaction to the violence, in which he called the white nationalists "some very fine people" and said that "both sides" were to blame for the bloody events.[5]

Near the end of the event, Acosta, CNN's chief White House correspondent and a veteran reporter with more than 20 years' experience covering national politics, questioned Trump about why it had taken him two days to condemn the white nationalist groups. (Disclosure: Jim Acosta was a colleague of mine when I worked at CNN's Washington Bureau from 2011 to 2015.)

Jim Acosta

> **Acosta:** *Mr. President, can you explain why you did not condemn those hate groups by name over the weekend?*

> **Trump:** *They've been condemned. They have been condemned.*

> **Acosta:** *Why are we not having a press conference today? You said on Friday we'd have a press conference.*

> **Trump:** *We had a press conference — we just had a press conference.*

> **Acosta:** *Can we ask you some more questions then, sir?*

> **Trump:** *It doesn't bother me at all, but you know I like real news, not fake news. [Points directly at CNN's cameras.] You're fake news.*

> **Acosta:** *[As Trump leaves the room] Haven't you spread a lot of fake news yourself, sir?*

President Donald Trump answers a question from CNN's Jim Acosta during a news conference announcing Alexander Acosta as the new Labor secretary nominee in the East Room at the White House on Feb. 16, 2017, in Washington, D.C.

It wasn't the first time Trump personally attacked Acosta and CNN. That was Jan. 11, 2017, nine days before Trump was sworn in as president.[6]

In a fiery, pre-inauguration press conference,[7] Trump was raging over a CNN report that classified documents originally given to President Barack Obama "included allegations that Russian operatives claimed to possess compromising personal and financial information about Trump." Trump went on a rant, first attacking BuzzFeed, which reported details of the so-called "dossier," calling the website a "failing pile of garbage."

Then he turned his attention to CNN.

> ***Trump:*** *And as far as CNN going out of their way to build it up... It's a disgrace, what took place. It's a disgrace. And I think they ought to apologize.*

Acosta: *Mr. president-elect, since you are attacking us, can you give us a question? Since you are attacking our news organization, can you give us a chance?*

Trump: *Not you... Not you. Your organization is terrible. Your organization is terrible. ... Quiet. Quiet. She's asking a question. Don't be rude. Don't. Be. Rude. No, I'm not going to give you a question. I'm not going to give you a question. You are fake news.*

Acosta: *Mr. president-elect, that is not appropriate.*

Acosta added that Sean Spicer, then Trump's press secretary and communications director, threatened to kick Acosta out of the briefing if he did it again.

The dossier was originally created by Fusion GPS for Democrats during the 2016 presidential campaign and was then turned over to the FBI. Recently, much of the dossier, compiled for Fusion by former British intelligence officer Christopher Steele, has been at least partially corroborated by the FBI and Justice Department officials, according to The Washington Post.[8]

But Trump is generous with his attacks on the media. One outlet has even called it Trump's "Fake Jihad Against the Fake News."[9]

Trump, apparently, doesn't care.

Donald J. Trump
@realDonaldTrump
So much Fake News being put in dying magazines and newspapers. Only place worse may be @NBCNews, @CBSNews, @ABC and @ CNN. Fiction writers!
5:51 PM - 17 Oct 2017

Over at NBC, the network, after reporting that Secretary of State Rex Tillerson had allegedly called the president a "moron" during a meeting at the Pentagon,[10] got the full force of Trump's anger on Twitter.

Donald J. Trump
@realDonaldTrump
NBC news is #FakeNews and more dishonest than even CNN. They
are a disgrace to good reporting. No wonder their news ratings are
way down!
7:47 AM - 4 Oct 2017

He continued to unload.

Donald J. Trump
@realDonaldTrump
The @NBCNews story has just been totally refuted by Sec. Tillerson
and @VP Pence. It is #FakeNews. They should issue an apology to
AMERICA!
8:18 AM - 4 Oct 2017

NBC stood by the story. And in a later interview, Tillerson refused to
deny that he called his boss a moron.[11]

But Trump doesn't think all in the media are bad. He routinely grants
interviews to "friendly" outlets such as Breitbart News, formerly run by his
former confidant Steve Bannon, or Fox News Channel, which he watches
regularly each morning in the residence on the third floor of the White
House.[12]

He has even said that some in the media — about one-third, which
roughly matches up to his approval rating — are actually decent folks.

While addressing a graduation at the FBI National Academy in Virginia,[13]
Trump directed everyone's attention to the traveling group of reporters,
producers, photographers, videographers and technicians — commonly
referred to as "the Pool" — gathered near the rear of the hall.

"But as I look out in the audience today, I see many young, bright faces.
To them, and to many other young Americans watching at home, of which
there are many — you see, there's the fake news back there. Look, everybody. Fake news. No, actually, some of them are fine people. About — let's
see, who's back there? Yeah, about 30 percent."

THE DEAD VOTERS OF BORDALAMA

In the days after Democrat Doug Jones' victory over Republican Roy Moore in the Alabama special election for the Senate seat vacated by Attorney General Jeff Sessions, a flurry of websites and social media posts reported that 5,329 dead people had voted for Jones in the small town of Bordalama, supposedly about 20 miles outside of Birmingham.

The website Ladies of Liberty ran a "story" on Dec. 14, 2017, with a headline proclaiming that "'Thousands' Voted for Doug Jones in Alabama Town With Population of 2,256":

More news about the corruption of the Democrat Party has surfaced — again related to the hotly contested Alabama special election to the Senate.

The State Election Board of Voting Integrity said early on that 'more than a third' of Jones' votes up to 11 a.m. looked suspicious — and with good reason. Many of them came from the small town of Bordalama, a rural community about 20 miles outside Birmingham.

Bill Clark/CQ Roll Call

Alabama Democrat Doug Jones celebrates his victory over Judge Roy Moore at the Sheraton in Birmingham, Ala., on Tuesday, Dec. 12, 2017.

According to official tallies, Roy Moore received 953 votes in the small town. Doug Jones received 5,327. If the disparity in numbers isn't enough to give you reason to smell something fishy, the population of the town should. There are 2,256 residents there and only 1,867 registered voters. In other words, more people voted for Doug Jones than even live in Bordalama.

According to city records, Reddit user MAGA4Ever points out, 'there are 3,460 people buried in the local Mount Peace Cemetery — the exact difference between Moore votes and registered voters.' This means that in Bordalama, Roy Moore got 953 votes legitimately and if every single other registered voter voted for Jones he'd have about 914 making him the loser.

But it wasn't true. A lie. A hoax.

Fake.

There's no such thing as the State Election Board of Voting Integrity in Alabama. There is no Reddit user named "MAGA4Ever."

There's not even a town called Bordalama in Alabama. Or anywhere else in the United States. There is, however, a store in Toledo, Spain, called "Bordalama" that sells work clothes and uniforms. A basic lab coat will run you about 30 euros. Shipping is extra.

The made-up story was picked up by the right-wing outlet Conservative Stamp and repeated on scores of other fringe websites and conservative chat groups, as well as Twitter and Facebook.[14]

But few who posted, re-posted or tweeted out the original piece bothered to notice the tiny type on the bottom of the Ladies of Liberty site:

PAY ATTENTION

sat·ire ~ 'sa tī(ə)r

noun

the use of humor, irony, exaggeration, OR ridicule to expose and criticize people's stupidity or vices, particularly in the context of contemporary politics and other topical issues. If you disagree with

*the definition of satire or have decided it is synonymous with "come-
dy," you should really just move along.*

Thankfully, this joke — Ladies of Liberty (LOL) is an outlet linked to a
network of other sites, with a "stated mission of making conservative social media users look foolish by inducing them to spread outlandish lies"
— was debunked by Snopes.com and several other fact-checking sites.[15]
The site, and others like it, is, according to PolitiFact, run by a 45-year-old
Little League umpire-turned-blogger from Maine, Christopher Blair, aka
"Busta Troll."[16] Blair said he created the parody site to "fool conservatives
with fake stories most people would find absurd."

Nevertheless, Blair's hoax had traveled around the globe a few times,
launched by those who were predisposed or preconditioned to accept the
underlying narrative. For them, the truth didn't matter. The lie was much
more comfortable, consistent with existing political beliefs.

It fit. It didn't matter that it was fake.

WE DON'T BELIEVE YOU

The national receptivity to made-up news has roots in a growing distrust of most media outlets and has been fertilized by a political polarization that has few believing anything that runs counter to their beliefs.

In a recent Politico/Morning Consult poll, almost half of those asked
— 46 percent — said they believe the news media simply makes up news
stories about Trump.[17] Almost half. And, when you look more closely, the
divide is even more pronounced along partisan lines:

> *More than three-quarters of Republican voters, 76 percent, think
> the news media invent stories about Trump and his administration,
> compared with only 11 percent who don't think so. Among Demo-
> crats, one-in-five think the media make up stories, but a 65 percent
> majority think they do not. Forty-four percent of independent*

voters think the media make up stories about Trump, and 31 percent think they do not.

And the mainstream media hasn't done itself any favors, either. Just look at recent mistakes, corrections, clarifications or retractions by the press, which collectively taint media credibility and feed the perception that journalists should not be trusted.

· In June 2017, three CNN investigative journalists — including a top editor — resigned after the network had to retract a story about a "Russian investment fund with ties to Trump officials."[18] The story specifically implicated Trump confidant (and later short-lived White House Communications Director) Anthony Scaramucci. "I did nothing wrong," Scaramucci said at the time.

· Veteran journalist Brian Ross of ABC News was suspended for four weeks without pay in December after he incorrectly reported that former National Security Adviser Michael Flynn was going to testify that Trump, while still a candidate, had personally directed him to secretly meet with Russian officials.[19] The network issued a correction the next day. "We deeply regret and apologize for the serious error we made yesterday," ABC said in a statement. "The reporting conveyed by Ross during the special report had not been fully vetted through our editorial standards process."[20]

· On the day of Trump's inauguration, Time magazine's White House correspondent, Zeke Miller, reported that a bust of Martin Luther King Jr. that had been present during the Obama administration had been removed from the Oval Office.[21] It hadn't. It was still there, just temporarily blocked by a door and a Secret Service agent. Miller later tweeted: "The MLK bust is still there. I looked for it in the oval 2x & didn't see it. My

apologies to my colleagues...This is on me, not my colleagues.
I've been doing everything I can to fix my error. My apologies."

· A reporter from The Washington Post, Dave Weigel, tweeted
out a photo of a sparse crowd at a Trump rally in Pensacola,
Florida. "Packed to the rafters," he said satirically in the post
with the picture. Trump claimed the photo was taken earlier
in the day, before much of the crowd had arrived. Weigel
quickly deleted the picture and tweet, and then apologized on
Twitter.[22]

And in December, CNN had to again correct an earlier story reporting
that an email about hacked Democratic National Committee documents
was sent to Trump campaign officials on Sept. 14, 2016, not Sept. 4, 2016,
a fact that significantly changed the context of the original story.[23] CNN
screwed up, and Trump made sure everyone knew.

> **Donald J. Trump**
> *@realDonaldTrump*
> *Fake News CNN made a vicious and purposeful mistake yesterday.*
> *They were caught red handed, just like lonely Brian Ross at ABC*
> *News (who should be immediately fired for his "mistake"). Watch*
> *to see if @CNN fires those responsible, or was it just gross incompe-*
> *tence?*
> **5:02 AM - 9 Dec 2017**

> **Donald J. Trump**
> *@realDonaldTrump*
> *CNN'S slogan is CNN, THE MOST TRUSTED NAME IN NEWS.*
> *Everyone knows this is not true, that this could, in fact, be a fraud*
> *on the American Public. There are many outlets that are far more*
> *trusted than Fake News CNN. Their slogan should be CNN, THE*
> *LEAST TRUSTED NAME IN NEWS!*
> **5:21 AM - 9 Dec 2017**

Reporters have been suspended, producers fired and apologies made. Each incident risks further eroding the confidence the public has in the fourth estate. Trump uses his social media megaphone to make sure his followers know about these failings of the media.

> **Donald J. Trump**
> *@realDonaldTrump*
> *Very little discussion of all the purposely false and defamatory*
> *stories put out this week by the Fake News Media. They are out*
> *of control - correct reporting means nothing to them. Major lies*
> *written, then forced to be withdrawn after they are exposed...a stain*
> *on America!*
> **1:18 PM - 10 Dec 2017**

However, from erroneous reports of the crowd size at the inauguration to bogus allegations about being wiretapped by his predecessor to unsubstantiated assertions of rampant voter fraud[24] to repeatedly questioning the authenticity of Obama's birth certificate,[25] Trump rarely corrects his own mistakes or apologizes for his own inaccuracies or misstatements.

THE WORLD IS WEARY

Outside of the United States, while foreign leaders in at least 15 countries are following Trump's lead and adopting his mantra of "fake news" to put down political resistance,[26] others appear to be growing tired of, as former British Prime Minister David Cameron called it, Trump's perilous "fake news act."

"When Donald Trump uses the term 'fake news' to describe CNN and the BBC, that is not just a questionable political tactic. It's actually dangerous," said Cameron during a lecture in London.[27]

"Let me put it like this. President Trump: 'Fake news' is not broadcasters criticizing you, it's Russian bots and trolls targeting your democracy ... pumping out untrue stories day after day, night after night."

And Cameron's successor, British Prime Minister Theresa May, hit Trump even harder.

Following the U.S. president's flurry of anti-Muslim postings that retweeted the views of British far-right and discredited nationalist Jayda Fransen of Britain First, May condemned Trump's spreading of racist propaganda.

"It is wrong for the president to have done this," May said in a statement.

Several news outlets in Britain, the United States and elsewhere have widely reported that there was no independent corroboration of the veracity of the videos. According to NBC News, the incendiary videos linked to in the tweet had already been dismissed as false:

> *The first video Trump shared claimed to show a Muslim migrant beating up a Dutch boy on crutches. The second was captioned, "Muslim destroys a statute of Virgin Mary," and the third read, "Islamist mob pushes teenage boy off roof and beats him to death!" NBC News could not verify Britain First's claims of what the videos showed.*[28]

Even the Dutch Embassy in Washington shot back at Trump, saying that the video supposedly featuring a Dutch boy was inaccurate. "Facts do matter," their officials posted on Twitter.

Netherlands Embassy
@NLintheUSA
.@realDonaldTrump Facts do matter. The perpetrator of the violent act in this video was born and raised in the Netherlands. He received and completed his sentence under Dutch law.
11:26 AM - 29 Nov 2017

But Trump quickly responded, firing back at May, the leader of America's closest ally.

Donald J. Trump
@realDonaldTrump
.@Theresa_May, don't focus on me, focus on the destructive Radical
Islamic Terrorism that is taking place within the United Kingdom.
We are doing just fine!
8:02 PM - Nov 29, 2017

During an impromptu interview later that day, his new press secretary, Sarah Sanders, offered an unusual spin on Trump's retweet of the unsubstantiated videos.

"Whether it's a real video, the threat is real. And that's what the president is talking about, that's what the president is focused on is dealing with those real threats and those are real no matter how you look at it," said Sanders.[29]

That same tactic — labeling critical comments as fake news — seems to work for other world leaders and dictators:

· Syrian President Bashar Assad said of a report condemning the deaths of more than 13,000 people in Syrian military prisons, "You can forge anything these days. We are living in a fake news era."[30]

· Philippines President Rodrigo Duterte, with Trump laughing out loud right next to him, called journalists covering the American president's Manilla visit "spies."[31]

· Venezuelan President Nicolás Maduro lamented to Russian TV about criticism of his regime. "This is what we call 'fake news' today, isn't it?"[32]

Domestically, Trump's opponents and allies alike worry that he is taking his "fake news" tactic too far. Republican Sen. John McCain, who is no friend of the president, has condemned Trump's overuse of the hammer of "fake news."

The president "must understand his harmful rhetoric only empowers repressive regimes to jail reporters & silence the truth," McCain wrote on Twitter.[33]

McCain earlier told NBC that nothing less than the future of democracy is at stake.[34]

"If you want to preserve — I'm very serious now — if you want to preserve democracy as we know it, you have to have a free and many times adversarial press," said McCain. "And without it, I am afraid that we would lose so much of our individual liberties over time. That's how dictators get started."

VOTER BEWARE

Snopes.com has compiled a list of some of the top actual fake news sites — from World News Daily Report to NewsBuzzDaily — that through deception, satire or straight-up sleight of hand, prey on the gullibility of users who believe just about anything they read on the internet.[35]

Especially if it fits with their political ideology — left or right.

Here are some tips to figure out whether what you're reading is factual or whether it feels like propaganda designed to elicit an emotional reaction:

1. **If something sounds too fantastic to believe, research it.** If you can find it on reputable news outlets — CNN, The New York Times or the Guardian — then it has a higher likelihood of being true.

2. **But don't stop there.** Use the respected fact-checking sites such as PolitiFact, Fact Checker from The Washington Post or others to double or triple check.

3. **Beware of posts on social media** — especially Facebook — that come from outlets that you've never heard of. Check them out before reposting or retweeting.

4. When you see or hear a story — even from an otherwise reputable news outlet — that is based on a single, anonymous source, be skeptical until you can corroborate it from two other independent outlets.

5. If you hear something said by one of those TV pundits, analysts or pontificators on cable news, take it with a grain of salt, unless the parent network has verified and reported it independently. Those folks aren't always bound by the same journalistic standards as real reporters.

6. And if Trump says a story is "fake news," that's a good indicator that it is probably (but not always), real, actual news. He just doesn't like it.

CHAPTER FOUR

The Psychology
Of Political Polarization
And Pessimism

By Michael Shermer

The Psychology of Political Polarization and Pessimism

N o one in history has ever joined a cult — they join a group they believe will be beneficial to themselves, to society or to both. In like manner, no one thinks that they belong to a political party — left or right — whose goal it is to destroy America, despite what members of the other party think about the intentions of their opposites. And, in my own field of science, no one in either party is self-consciously anti-science, blatantly denying evidence everyone else can see is valid, nor does anyone engage in pseudoscience or think that their beliefs are supported by pseudo-facts collected in pseudo-laboratories in support of pseudo-theories.[1]

In fact, most people think that their political beliefs are logical and sound, and nearly everyone embraces science and recognizes that we live in the Age of Science, which is why even extreme political ideologues on both the right and the left attempt to at least ground their science-related beliefs in evidence and reason. It's also why most of us unconcernedly board jet aircraft, use cellphones, watch television and listen to radio, heed tornado warnings, acknowledge earthquakes as the product of plate tectonics and not angry gods, and accept the germ theory of disease and visit physicians and imbibe pharmaceuticals rather than burn witches.

A similar asymmetry can be found in how we evaluate the status of our society: it seems like things are bad and getting worse when, in fact, they are good and getting better. Why do we misperceive our society in this manner? Because of a cognitive quirk of the human mind called the "availability bias," in which we tend to assign probabilities of potential outcomes based on examples that are immediately available to us, especially those that are vivid, unusual or emotionally salient.[2] For example, our initial assessment of what is most likely to kill us — terrorist bombings, shark attacks, earthquakes, hurricanes, lightning strikes, police brutality, killer bees — is whatever happens to be on the evening news at the time we're thinking about it. With our focus on headlines instead of trend lines, our intuitions lead us to conclude that the world is going to hell in a handbasket. Syria, Russia, Crimea, North Korea, Trump, Brexit, terrorism, police shootings, and especially political polarization, make it seem as if we are living in the worst of times. Has all the political, economic and social progress The United States has achieved over the past several centuries — the abolition of slavery, the decline in rates of homicides, crime and violence, the expansion of the moral sphere to include civil rights, women's rights, children's rights, worker's rights, and gay rights for more people in more places — been suddenly erased? Are we lurching backwards to the time when bigots burned women at the stake as witches? In a word: No!

In my 2015 book "The Moral Arc," I explained how science played a significant role in all this moral progress,[3] and an even more poignant example can be found in an April 2016 speech in which then President Barack Obama asked rhetorically, "If you had to choose a moment in time to be born, any time in human history, and you didn't know ahead of time what nationality you were or what gender or what your economic status might be," what time would you choose? Would it be Ancient Greece or Rome? Medieval times? Elizabethan England? Colonial America? The 1950s?

"You'd choose today," Obama answered his own question. "We're fortunate to be living in the most peaceful, most prosperous, most progressive era in human history," adding "that it's been decades since the last war between major powers. More people live in democracies. We're wealthier and healthier and better educated, with a global economy that has lifted up more than a billion people from extreme poverty."[4]

He's right. Data aggregated and graphed by the economist Max Roser on his site ourworldindata.org, along with that compiled from the World Bank, the United Nations, the Organisation for Economic Co-operation and Development (OECD) and Eurostat available at humanprogress.org, show unquestionably that we are living in the best epoch of human history.

To say that the past 10 years was the best decade in the history of our species sounds hallucinatory to most people, but the trend lines all show that such a view is supported by the facts. The vast majority of the 100 billion people who came before us, for example, lived in what would today be considered abject poverty. The top one-percenters of centuries past possessed next to none of the comforts and indulgences that the typical middle-class Westerner enjoys today: medical and dental care, public health measures and medicine; homes with heating and air conditioning, refrigeration, gas or electric stoves, dish washers, washer-dryer units and other creature comforts; over 10 billion products from which to choose at supermarkets, warehouse outlets and online stores; national and international jet travel allowing a traveler to go anywhere in the world in a matter of hours; wireless communications with anyone, anywhere, anytime; and of course internet access to all the world's knowledge, largely at no cost. All this prosperity would have been unimaginable to our immediate ancestors and inconceivable to anyone who lived centuries or millennia ago.[5]

NEGATIVITY BIAS

There are a number of other psychological factors at work that make it seem as if conditions in our society are moving in the wrong direction. As I document in my 2018 book "Heavens on Earth," these factors involve features of both human cognition and social life.[6] First, news media outlets are far more likely to report bad news than good, simply because that is what they've been tasked to do. Another day in Sweden without political unrest goes unreported, but just try to annex a portion of Ukraine without the world's media covering it. Second, the social psychologist Roy Baumeister identified a deeper program in our psychology called the "negativity bias," which he described as "Bad Is Stronger Than Good," the title of the 2001 paper he co-authored in the Review of General Psychology.[7] In an analysis of over 17,000 psychological research papers, 69 percent of them dealt with negative issues compared with only 31 percent that focused on positive issues. That is because bad things have a greater impact on human thought and behavior than do good, so it is easier to analyze because there are bigger size effects and thus the results are more likely to get funded and published.

> "*Bad emotions, bad parents and bad feedback have more impact than good ones, and bad information is processed more thoroughly than good.*"

"Bad emotions, bad parents and bad feedback have more impact than good ones, and bad information is processed more thoroughly than good," the authors concluded. "Bad impressions and bad stereotypes are quicker to form and more resistant to disconfirmation than good ones." For example: Bad smells elicit far more animated facial expressions than good or neutral odors; bad impressions and negative stereotypes form faster and are more resistant to change than positive ones; memory recall is better for bad behaviors, events and information than it is for good; losing money and friends has a greater impact on people than gaining money and friends; criticism and negative feedback hurt more than praise and positive feedback feels good.

Why are we programmed in this fashion? One answer, I suggest, is in the psychology of "loss aversion," in which, on average, losses hurt twice as much as gains feel good. In the investment world, to get someone to take a gamble on an investment, the potential payoff must be about twice the potential loss. The classic experiment in the effect was conducted by economist Richard Thaler, recent recipient of the Nobel Prize for his pioneering work in behavioral economics. He gave subjects a coffee mug valued at $6 and asked them what they would sell it for. The average price was $5.25. Another group of subjects were asked how much they would pay for the same mug. The average price was $2.75. About half. We value more what we already have, and losing it is doubly painful.[8]

The effect is pronounced in sports. Tennis champion Jimmy Connors put it this way in a 1975 Sports Illustrated article: "I hate losing more than I love winning."[9] Cycling superstar Lance Armstrong echoed the sentiment in explaining to filmmaker Alex Gibney that he was more motivated to not let cancer — and subsequently other cyclists — defeat him, than he was by the pull of the positive payoffs of winning (which were substantial for him): "I like to win, but more than anything, I can't stand this idea of losing. Because to me, losing means death."[10]

What can we do to combat the negativity bias in the news? First, follow the trend lines and not just the headlines, and ask how the daily news stories fit into larger long-term patterns of change. Second, periodically check with the aforementioned sites humanprogress.org and ourworldindata.org, along with Snopes.com and Skeptic.com for debunking myths and detecting false stories. Third, follow FactCheck.org, OpenSecrets.org and PolitiFact.com, sites that fact-check the speeches and statements of politicians, the latter site waggishly ranking political claims as True, Mostly True, Half True, Mostly False and Pants on Fire.

Another answer to the way our psychology is wired is evolution.

In the world in which our ancestors evolved their cognition and emotions that we inherited, there were more ways for things to go bad than good, so our modern psychology is tuned to a world that was more dangerous in our evolutionary past than it is today. In a complex machine or body, for example, all the parts must consistently work to keep the thing going, but if one part or system fails it can be catastrophic to all the other parts and systems if the machine or organism stops or dies. Stability of the overall system must be maintained, which requires the brain running the system to devote the most attention to threats that could terminate the organism. You only live as long as everything works, so the good news of, say, experiencing yet another day of your heart steadily beating goes unnoticed, but a nonfatal cardiac arrest focuses the mind on this single bad event. There are many ways that things can go south quickly, and this creates an asymmetry between optimism and pessimism, with the latter stronger than the former.[11]

TRIBALISM AND POLITICAL POLARIZATION

Another feature of our psychology that helps explain both our pessimism and our political polarization is "tribalism," and its effects can be seen in how predictable we are on political, economic and social issues. For example, if you are a conservative, I predict that you watch Fox News; read the Wall Street Journal; listen to conservative talk radio; love the former George Bushes (H.W. and W.); voted for President Donald Trump; despise former Vice President Al Gore and consider Obama to be a socialist; are anti-immigration, pro-life and anti-gun control; believe that America is a Christian nation that should meld church and state; are against universal health care; vote against measures to redistribute wealth and tax the rich; and are skeptical of global warming. If you are a liberal, I predict that you watch CNN or PBS; listen to NPR; read The New York Times; loathe the Bushes (especially W.); consider former GOP vice presidential nominee Sarah Palin to be an imbecile; admire Gore and revere Obama; are pro-immigration, pro-choice and anti-gun; adhere to the separation of church and state; are in favor of universal health care; vote for measures to redistribute wealth and tax the rich in order to level the playing field; and believe that global warming is real, human caused and potentially disastrous for civilization if the government doesn't do something dramatic and soon. Most of us in our political lives are so predictable that if I know just one of your positions on these many seemingly independent issues, I can discern the others, indicating how closely clustered they are into these ideological boxes. If, for example, I know your position on abortion — anti-abortion or pro-abortion rights — I can predict with great certainty your position on most of these other key issues.

Why do we divide ourselves into these political tribes? According to political scientists Donald Green, Bradley Palmquist and Eric Schickler in their book "Partisan Hearts and Minds," most people do not select a political party because it reflects their views; instead, they first identify with a political position, usually inherited from their parents (both genetically and environmentally), peer groups, and upbringing, then once they have made a commitment to that political position they choose the party that best fits it. This is the power of political tribalism, and we all know the stereotypes that each tribe holds about members of the other tribe. Here, for example, is my characterization of what conservatives think of liberals:

> *Liberals are a bunch of hybrid-driving, tofu-eating, tree-hugging, whale-saving, sandal-wearing, big-government promoting, tax increasing, bottled-water-drinking, flip-flopping, wishy-washy, namby-pamby bedwetters.*

And this is what liberals think of conservatives:

> *Conservatives are a bunch of Hummer-driving, meat-eating, gun-toting, small-government promoting, tax decreasing, hard-drinking, Bible-thumping, black-and-white-thinking, fist-pounding, shoe-stomping, morally dogmatic blowhards.*

Such stereotypes exaggerate any one person's beliefs, of course, which is why we should never judge individuals based on group characteristics. But stereotypes do often contain an element of truth in them that, in this case, reflects an emphasis on differing moral values, especially those we derive intuitively.

To combat these stereotypes, the best thing any of us can do is to diversify our sources of information, including and especially politically. Don't just consume news from sources supporting your political preferences. If you are a liberal, force yourself to periodically pick up (or log on to) the Wall Street Journal and read its editorials. If you are a conservative, bite your lip and open The New York Times and turn to its op-ed section to see what people in the other tribe are thinking. You might learn something new, but if nothing else, it will at least strengthen your own position by better knowing what opponents of it are arguing.

CONFIRMATION BIAS

In fact, research now overwhelming demonstrates that most of our moral decisions are grounded in automatic moral feelings rather than deliberatively rational calculations. We do not reason our way to a moral decision by carefully weighing the evidence for and against; instead, we make intuitive leaps to moral decisions, and then after the fact we rationalize the snap decision with rational reasons. Our moral intuitions — reflected in such conservative-liberal stereotypes — are more emotional than rational. These are then reinforced by another cognitive bug called the "confirmation bias" — the tendency to seek and find confirming evidence in support of already existing beliefs and ignore or reinterpret disconfirming evidence. Experimental examples abound:

> · In 1981, the psychologist Mark Snyder tasked subjects to assess the personality of someone whom they were about to meet, but only after they reviewed a written profile of the person. One group of subjects was given a profile of an introvert (shy, timid, quiet), while another group was given a profile of an extrovert (sociable, talkative, outgoing). When asked to make a personality assessment, those subjects who were told that the person would be an extrovert tended to ask questions that would lead to that conclusion; the introvert group did the same in the opposite direction.[12]

· In a 1983 study, the psychologists John Darley and Paul Gross showed subjects a video of a child taking a test. One group was told that the child was from a high socioeconomic class, while the other group was told that the child was from a low socioeconomic class. The subjects were then asked to evaluate the academic abilities of the child based on the results of the test. Even though both groups of subjects were evaluating the exact same set of numbers, those who were told that the children they were evaluating were from a high socioeconomic class rated the child's abilities as above grade level, and those who thought that the kids were from a low socioeconomic class rated the kids as below grade level in ability. It's another example of the "Pygmalion effect," in which higher expectations lead to an increase in performance.[13]

I argued in my 2011 book "The Believing Brain" that confirmation bias is most notable in political beliefs, particularly the manner in which our belief filters allow in information that confirms our ideological convictions and filters out information that disconfirms those same convictions.[14] This is why it is so easy to predict which media outlets liberals and conservatives choose to monitor, and social media sites such as Facebook and Twitter only throw fuel on the confirmation bias fire.

An elegant study conducted at Emory University by the psychologist Drew Westen included a brain scan of subjects during the run-up to the 2004 presidential election. After sliding subjects into an fMRI machine, 30 men — half of whom described themselves as "strong" Republicans and the other half as "strong" Democrats — were tasked with assessing statements by both Republican incumbent George W. Bush and Democratic Sen. John Kerry in which the candidates clearly contradicted themselves. As predicted by the confirmation bias, in their assessments of the candidates Republican subjects were as critical of Kerry as Democratic subjects were of Bush, yet both let their own preferred candidate off the hook when exposed to their contradictions.[15]

What was especially revealing were the brain scan results: the part of the brain most associated with reasoning — the dorsolateral prefrontal cortex — was dark and inactive compared to the orbital frontal cortex, which is involved in the processing of emotions. Revealingly, once subjects had arrived at a conclusion that made them emotionally comfortable, their ventral striatum became active, a part of the brain associated with reward. In other words, instead of rationally evaluating a candidate's positions on this or that issue, or analyzing the planks of each candidate's platform, we have an emotional reaction to conflicting data, in which we rationalize away the parts that do not fit our preconceived beliefs about a candidate, then receive a reward in the form of a neurochemical hit, probably dopamine.

As with most of our beliefs about most things in life, our moral beliefs come first, and the rationalization of those moral beliefs comes second. In his book "The Righteous Mind: Why Good People Are Divided by Politics and Religion," psychologist Jonathan Haidt contends that most of our political and religious beliefs are grounded in five innate and universally available psychological systems that conservatives and liberals emphasize in differing amounts:

1. **Harm/care,** related to our long evolution as mammals with attachment systems and an ability to feel (and dislike) the pain of others. This foundation underlies virtues of kindness, gentleness and nurturance.

2. **Fairness/reciprocity,** related to the evolutionary process of reciprocal altruism. This foundation generates ideas of justice, rights and autonomy.

3. **Ingroup/loyalty,** related to our long history as tribal primates able to form shifting coalitions. This foundation underlies virtues of patriotism and self-sacrifice for the group.

4. **Authority/respect,** shaped by our long history of hierarchical social interactions. This foundation underlies virtues of

leadership and followership, including deference to legitimate authority and respect for traditions.

5. Purity/sanctity, shaped by the psychology of disgust and contamination. This foundation underlies religious notions of striving to live in an elevated, less carnal, more noble way. It underlies the widespread idea that the body is a temple that can be desecrated by immoral activities and contaminants (an idea also found in some political traditions).[16]

Over the years Haidt and his colleagues have surveyed hundreds of thousands of people from around the world and found this consistent difference between liberals and conservatives: Liberals are higher than conservatives on 1 and 2 (Harm/care and Fairness/reciprocity), but lower than conservatives on 3, 4 and 5 (Ingroup/loyalty, Authority/respect and Purity/sanctity). Conservatives are roughly equal on all five dimensions, lower than liberals on 1 and 2 but higher on 3, 4 and 5. (You can take the survey yourself at yourmorals.org.)

In other words, liberals question authority, celebrate diversity, often flaunt faith and tradition in order to care for the weak and oppressed, and they want change and justice even at the risk of political and economic chaos. By contrast, conservatives emphasize institutions and traditions, faith and family, nation and creed, and they want order even at the cost of those at the bottom falling through the cracks. Of course, there are exceptions to such generalizations, but the point is that instead of viewing the left and the right as either right or wrong (depending on which one you are), a more reflective approach is to recognize that liberals and conservatives emphasize different moral values and tend to sort themselves into these two clusters.

To work around these tendencies we all have, an excellent resource is the Heterodox Academy, a group of academics devoted to viewpoint diversity founded by Haidt and his colleagues (I am a member) to combat the growing problem of political bias on college and university campuses, particularly among faculty members in the humanities and social sciences, where Democrat to Republican ratios can be as high as 10 to one or even 20 to one, depending on the department. Heterodox-academy.org has many resources on how to expand viewpoint diversity among students and faculty by inviting speakers whose politics or social attitudes are different from most people on campus, by assigning readings of authors who do not fit the stereotype of one's preferred opinions, by sharing opinion essays by writers who will provoke us to think outside of our ideological boxes. As the academy's resolution states: "Research shows that the kind of diversity that most improves the quality and creativity of thinking is viewpoint diversity. When everyone thinks alike, there is a danger of groupthink, prejudice, dogmatism, and orthodoxy. People in the majority benefit from interacting with individuals who see things differently."[17]

POLITICAL TRIBES AND FACTS

All of these psychological factors are at work in explaining how our political tribes distort facts and the news, especially related to science.

That conservatives doubt scientific findings and theories that conflict with their political and religious beliefs, for example, is evident from even a cursory scan of right-leaning media. Creationism and the denial of evolution that has disrupted science education programs in public schools; the anti-vaccination movement that has led to the return of communicable diseases in communities where enough parents chose not to vaccinate their children that the herd immunity wall was breached; the delay of stem cell research because of religious beliefs about the sanctity of life, even a 16-cell blastoma consisting of immature and undifferentiated cells; and the denial of human-caused global climate change, in which the scientific consensus of 97 percent of peer-reviewed papers collided with politics, are the most egregious examples in recent decades.

Polls bear out the bias. A 2012 Gallup poll, for example, found that "58 percent of Republicans believe that God created humans in their present form within the last 10,000 years," compared with 41 percent of Democrats.[18] A 2011 survey by the Public Religion Research Institute found that 81 percent of Democrats but only 49 percent of Republicans believe that Earth is getting warmer.[19]

The left's war on science begins with the stats cited above: 41 percent of Democrats are young Earth creationists and 19 percent doubt that Earth is getting warmer. These numbers do not exactly bolster the common belief that liberals are the people of science. That liberals are just as guilty of anti-science bias is surprising to most academics and scientists, and yet those on the left are skeptical of well-established science when findings clash with their political ideologies on issues like genetically modified food, nuclear power, genetic engineering and evolutionary psychology. (I've called rejection of the latter "cognitive creationism" for its endorsement of a blank slate model of the mind in which natural selection operated on humans only from the neck down.) There's more, and recent, anti-science from far-left progressives, documented in the 2012 book "Science Left Behind" by science journalists Alex B. Berezow and Hank Campbell, who note that "if it is true that conservatives have declared a war on science, then progressives have declared Armageddon."[20]

On energy issues, for example, the authors contend that progressive liberals tend to be anti-nuclear because of the waste disposal problem, anti-fossil fuels because of global warming, anti-hydroelectric because dams disrupt river ecosystems and anti-wind power because of avian fatalities. The underlying current is "everything natural is good" and "everything unnatural is bad." The left's sacred values are focused primarily on the environment, leading to an almost religious fervor over the purity and sanctity of air, water and especially food. Try having a conversation with a liberal progressive about genetically modified organisms, or GMOs, and you'll hear the words "Monsanto profit" and "evil" dropped like syllogistic bombs. The fact is we've been genetically modifying organisms for 10,000 years through breeding and selection. It's the only way to feed billions of people.

Such anti-science attitudes not only form along these political tribal lines, they are found in only a very narrow strip of belief: those in which certain scientific findings or theories appear to oppose specific political or religious views.

According to the psychologist Asheley Landrum, an expert on factors that influence the public understanding and perception of science, over 90 percent of both Republicans and Democrats agreed in polls that "science and technology give more opportunities" and that "science makes our lives better." Revealingly, she also shows that the modest effect of the "Knowledge Deficit Hypothesis," in which more knowledge about a topic leads to greater acceptance of it — for example, those who know more about climate science are slightly more likely to accept that global warming is real and caused by humans than those who know less on the subject — is completely erased when political ideology is factored in. For example, the more knowledge Republicans have about climate science the less likely they are to accept the theory of anthropogenic global warming, or AGW. By contrast, and predictably, the more knowledge Democrats have on climate change the more confidence they have in the theory of AGW. As Landrum explained: "People with more knowledge only accept science when it doesn't conflict with their pre-existing beliefs and values. Otherwise, they use that knowledge to more strongly justify their own positions."[21]

In a 2017 paper published in the Journal of Risk Research titled "Culturally Antagonistic Memes and the Zika Virus," Landrum and her colleagues demonstrated the effect experimentally.[22] They first had participants read a news story on Zika public health risks that was linked to either climate change or immigration. Predictably, when Zika was connected to climate change there was an increase in concern among Democrats and a decrease in concern among Republicans, but when Zika was associated with immigration the effects were reversed — suddenly Republicans became concerned and Democrats disinterested. In other words, their skepticism was not applied equally across the board — it was dependent on context. Landrum explained the psychological phenomenon at work: "We are good at being skeptical when information conflicts with our pre-existing beliefs and values. We are bad at being skeptical when information is compatible with our pre-existing beliefs and values."

COGNITIVE DISSONANCE

There is one final psychological factor that distorts our thinking on important political issues and further polarizes the country: "cognitive dissonance."

In his classic 1964 book "When Prophecy Fails," psychologist Leon Festinger described what happened to a UFO cult when the alien mothership failed to arrive at the appointed date and time. Instead of admitting error and returning to their normal lives, "members of the group sought frantically to convince the world of their beliefs," and they made "a series of desperate attempts to erase their rankling dissonance by making prediction after prediction in the hope that one would come true."[23] Festinger called this cognitive dissonance, defining it as the uncomfortable tension that comes from holding two conflicting thoughts at the same time. Two of his students, Carol Tavris and Elliot Aronson, in their 2007 book "Mistakes Were Made (but not by me)," document thousands of experiments demonstrating how people spin facts to fit preconceived beliefs in order to reduce dissonance. Their metaphor of the "pyramid of choice" places two individuals side by side at the apex of the pyramid and shows how quickly they diverge and end up at the bottom opposite corners of the base as they each stake out a position to defend.[24]

An example of cognitive dissonance at work in the political arena is in the "backfire effect," so labeled by the psychologists Brendan Nyhan and Jason Reifler, based on a series of experiments they conducted "in which corrections actually increase misperceptions among the group in question." Why? "Because it threatens their worldview or self-concept."[25]

For example, subjects were given fake newspaper articles that confirmed widespread misconceptions, such as that there were weapons of mass destruction in Iraq. When subjects were then given a corrective article that WMDs were never found, liberals who opposed the war accepted the new article and rejected the old, whereas conservatives who supported the war did the opposite — and more: They reported being even more convinced there were WMDs after the correction, arguing that this only proved that Saddam Hussein hid or destroyed them. In fact, Nyhan and

Reifler noted, among many conservatives "the belief that Iraq possessed WMD immediately before the U.S. invasion persisted long after the Bush administration itself concluded otherwise." As Tavris told me when I queried her about this:

> *In short, there simply is massive evidence that the primary justification for going into Iraq was wrong. That creates dissonance for people who supported the war and believed President Bush — which was as many Democrats as Republicans at the outset. In our book, we are careful to note that both Republicans and Democrats reduced dissonance about their early support for the war being based on WMD, but they did it differently: Many Republicans refused to accept the evidence that there were no WMD, and many Democrats "forgot" they ever supported the war.*[26]

AVOIDING THE BACKFIRE EFFECT

What can we do to combat the backfire effect and its deeper psychological variable cognitive dissonance, along with our political polarization and pessimism? In a career devoted to studying beliefs and engaging people in public debates and dialogues, most notably those of a different persuasion from myself on any number of topics, I suggest a number of steps we can all take:

1. **Keep emotions out of the exchange;** emotions cloud judgment and rationality and only ramp up the emotions of those on the other side.

2. **Discuss, don't attack** — no reductio ad hominem, and especially no reductio ad hitlerem! The moment you call someone a Nazi, or accuse them of being fascists, the conversation is over and the battle has begun.

3. Listen carefully and try to articulate the other position accurately. This is an old debate rule: restate your opponent's position until they agree that you've captured it perfectly. Even if you disagree with it, it shows that you're at least paying attention.

4. Show respect. Everyone wants to be respected. The moment you roll your eyes, snort or sniff or mumble under your breath when the other person is speaking, the cognitive dissonance wall goes up.

5. Acknowledge that you understand why someone might hold that opinion, and all the better if you've actually once held that position because it shows empathy.

6. Be willing to change your mind, to say "I don't know" and "I could be wrong."

7. Try to show how changing facts does not necessarily mean changing worldviews. If someone thinks that in order to accept some narrow scientific fact it means giving up a deep political belief, religious tenet or moral foundation, the facts are likely to be defenestrated forthright. If you tell an evangelical that they have to choose between Darwin and Jesus, the carpenter will win every time. If you tell a Christian that evolution was God's way of creating life, they are more likely to accept the science behind Darwin's theory. Likewise with climate change. When conservatives hear the words "global warming," they turn them into "anti-capitalism" or "big government." Convince them that there need be no conflict between the science of AGW and the economics of free market, and they'll join you in saving the environment, especially if they can make a fortune investing in green technology.

These steps may not always work to counter our own cognitive dissonances and tribalism, but they may help us be better — more open to different opinions, less biased ourselves — at consuming news and information in a way that improves our ability to differentiate real from fake information.

CHAPTER FIVE

Algorithms: What Drives Our Filter Bubbles?

By Joshua Benton

Algorithms: What Drives
Our Filter Bubbles?

T he weekend before the 2016 presidential election, while Donald
Trump and Hillary Clinton were jetting around the country trying
to close the deal with voters, I was on Facebook. I'm from the
small town of Rayne, Louisiana, and I'd just seen one of my relatives share
a post from the mayor there. It wasn't an update on street repairs or an announcement of a new event at the RV park. It was: "Hillary Clinton Calling
for Civil War If Trump Is Elected."

I looked at what the mayor had been sharing over the previous few days
and there was a theme:

> "Pope Francis Shocks World, Endorses Donald Trump
> for President"

> "Barack Obama Admits He Was Born in Kenya"

> "FBI Agent Who Was Suspected of Leaking Hillary's Corrup-
> tion Is Dead"

"Breaking: Hillary Clinton Indicted, Prayers Answered"

"John Podesta's Satanic Dinner (Warning: Graphic Content)."

I looked through the comments on his posts and didn't see any fact checks, disagreements or even mild pushback. A number of the same phony stories showed up on the feeds of other people I knew back home, along with others that would soon be canonized as classics of the fake-news genre:

"Just Read the Law: Hillary Is Disqualified From Holding Any Federal Office"

"WikiLeaks Confirms Hillary Sold Weapons to ISIS"

"Nasty Surprise: Obama Told Americans That Their Freedom Is Over"

"New World Government Is Taking Over."

I live in Cambridge, Massachusetts, and I can assure you there was a substantial gap between what my friends in Cambridge and those back home were posting on Facebook around Election Day.

With the surprise Trump win that followed, it was clear that, alongside the many other divides carving up the American electorate, some of us were living in entirely different information universes, seemingly driven by Facebook's black-box algorithms. As noted in Chapter One, the late Sen. Daniel Patrick Moynihan's famous line held that everyone is entitled to his own opinion, but not his own facts. Facebook seemed, for at least a moment, like an existential threat to that idea.

During the Obama–Trump transition period, the rise of phony stories and deliberate "fake news" was a convenient boogie man for those trying to explain an election result they didn't like — or, in the case of the news media, trying to explain why their reporting hadn't prepared their audiences for it. With an election decided by such a narrow margin, it was possible to blame (or credit) just about anything for shifting the crucial votes. It remains unclear the degree to which voters' minds were changed by socially distributed misinformation; I doubt my hometown's mayor would have been a Clinton voter in any case. But the larger questions that emerged about Facebook in particular — and algorithmically curated news in general — have lingered.

THE PROMISE AND PERIL OF DIGITAL OPTIMIZATION

An algorithm is a set of rules used to solve a problem in a number of steps. Your grandma's green-bean casserole recipe is an algorithm; so is the unspoken set of decisions you make getting ready to head out the door in the morning. (Is it raining? Grab the umbrella. Is it windy and cold? Put on the scarf.)

But the algorithms that seem to dominate every corner of our digital lives are a lot more complicated. Or, at a minimum, they operate at a far greater scale — a scale that turns simple decision-making into something more abstract and Borg-like. How does Google know what search result to show me, which email to declare a priority or what YouTube video is most likely to occupy my next three minutes? How does Amazon know that I'll like that duvet cover so much? How does Facebook take a nearly boundless universe of timely information — wedding videos, dank memes, Instagram brunch photos, news from Syria — and pick which meet my scrolling thumb first? The answer to each is an algorithm.

For the world's modern tech giants, the important data that feeds these algorithms comes from the users themselves. Our past clicks and taps serve as ephemeral votes, saying "I like that, give me more." The power of that feedback loop — data leads to better outputs, which leads to more usage, which leads to more data — is what has allowed a few companies in Northern California to become goliaths on an almost unimaginable scale.

In most cases, when one of these companies gets very good at optimizing for what we like, it doesn't seem like a bad thing. It's hard to object when Spotify does a really great job at assembling a playlist based on its knowledge of every song you've played or skipped before. If Amazon sees I've recently purchased a bed, a set of sheets, a couple pillows and a duvet, the fact that it can then recommend that duvet cover might even qualify as an actual service.

The stakes are a little different when it comes to news, though. "News you'll really like" isn't the same as "news that's accurate and important." Algorithms are pretty good at delivering the former, but sometimes at the expense of the latter. And the potential impacts of this sort of over-optimization on democracy are more important than whatever happens to the duvet cover industry.

"'News you'll really like' isn't the same as 'news that's accurate and important.'"

Consider the inputs a good editor might consider when deciding whether a story is important enough to be put on the home page or to lead an evening newscast. She would have contextual knowledge of the main players involved in the piece; she would know the quality of prior work done by the journalists involved in its production; she would know what stories have been done on the subject before. And she'd have years of experience making exactly these sorts of decisions, over and over again, learning what worked and what didn't for the editorial approach of her news organization.

That's not to say that editors are perfect. She might also rely on inputs like her own personal biases, her mood in a morning meeting or what her boss keeps bugging her to feature. And while I'm using the female pronoun in this example, most editors are male, white, college-educated and middle class or higher — each of which can serve as its own set of editorial blinders.

But the data available to an editorial algorithm is generally limited to the quantitative. At its most elemental, an algorithm may treat a URL as just a string of letters, drawing no more meaning from it than it would from the ingredients list of a cupcake recipe or a string of random characters. A more common level of sophistication would allow an algorithm knowledge of how an article has been, to use the coin of the realm, "engaged" with — meaning how it has been liked, faved, shared, commented upon or otherwise fiddled with within the confines of its platform.

In some cases, algorithmic systems can access somewhat more sophisticated data — how long an article was being read or at least scrolled through, whether others have reported it as abusive, reputational data about the article's publisher or even whether an independent fact-checking organization has declared its pants to be on fire.

But in general, at the scale required by large social platforms, the inputs determining any given article's rank or placement will be driven primarily by the most straightforward indications of engagement, ham-fisted as they are.

At Facebook's developer conference in 2016, the company's vice president in charge of News Feed, Adam Mosseri, laid out how the company thought about the process.[1] Using his own feed as an example, for any given piece of content, "We try to figure out how likely am I, Adam, to like this story, to share this story, to spend time reading this story," he said. "These sorts of actions we think of as proxies to knowing that I'm interested in this story."[1]

If two potential posts are competing for a spot in someone's News Feed, Mosseri said, "and one has thousands of likes and comments, and the other only has, like, three or four, we're going to infer that the former is much more interesting than the latter."

But were lots of people liking that article because it was great investigative journalism or because it was something so awful it became an entertaining hate-read? Were all those comments driven by an earnest discussion of policy preferences or because the rest of the family had to gang up on Uncle Jeff for sharing racist memes again? Were those shares rewarding quality reporting or giving digital thanks for creating a piece of content so perfectly pleasing to those rooting for a certain political team?

Even within a single genre of user action, any number of potential motivations could prove to be the trigger. Does a like mean "I'm happy that the event described in this article happened" — or "I think this is a good article even if it's about something I don't enjoy"? Two quite different intentions, folded into a single data point for the algorithm to crunch.

CONCERNS ABOUT ALGORITHMIC EDITING

Some of the early concerns about algorithmic editing arrived in public discourse around 2011, when Eli Pariser's book "The Filter Bubble" was published. His primary illustration of the risk at hand was the personalization of Google search results leading to different people getting different results for the same keywords. One person's search for "BP" might show the energy company's stock price; another's might direct him to information about the Deepwater Horizon oil spill.

Critics at the time disputed the extent of the issue (some found Google's personalization to have only minor effects), and some researchers argued that a social network like Facebook actually exposed users to a broader range of perspectives than they would otherwise see.[2] After all, the proper point of comparison to Facebook isn't some ideal of Athenian democracy or a New England town meeting; it's the messy, imperfect set of political conversations that we'd be having if the internet didn't exist. The friends we talk to about news in real life tend to be like us; yes, Facebook included those people, but also that weird kid with the fedora from high school, that great-aunt you see once every five years and other people with whom you have weaker ties.

But that was before Facebook grew from an important social network into the largest real-time distributor of human attention the world has ever known. By 2012, 49 percent of Americans reported seeing news on social media, according to the Pew Research Center; by 2017, that was up to 67 percent. The internet has far surpassed print and radio as a source of news for Americans, and it has nearly caught up with television. And Facebook is the driving force behind much of that growth; more than twice as many Americans say they get news from Facebook than from any other social media platform. By 2016, its users worldwide were spending an astonishing 50 minutes per day using Facebook products.[3]

That enormous scale raised the stakes in several ways. Facebook became the number one provider of traffic to many, if not most, online news sites. Newsrooms built teams dedicated to posting and promoting their work on the platform. Tweaks in Facebook's algorithm could bring publishers either traffic glory or revenue collapse.

Any algorithm that produces outcomes sufficiently important to people will eventually be gamed. In the early 2000s, Google searches became so dominant a driver of web traffic that an entire multibillion-dollar industry — search engine optimization, or SEO — sprang up to try to manipulate it for money. Newsroom gurus started swapping tips about keyword density and backlinks to build PageRank — all in the hopes of moving from the 12th result on a search results page to the first.

And as Facebook grew, the art and science of social media optimization grew alongside it. Headlines moved from declarative to teasing; giving away too much on Facebook might obviate the need for a further click. Stories began to promise "you won't believe what happened next." Calls for comments and engagement — key to the algorithm — became more explicit.

> *"'I saw it on Facebook' is the new 'I read it in the Times.'"*

But above all other factors driving algorithmic virality stood emotion. The emotion could be joy or inspiration ("21 Pictures That Will Restore Your Faith in Humanity," slideshows of puppies). It could be anger or disgust ("You Won't Believe the Terrible Thing [Political Opponent] Has Done Now"). A post that didn't provoke any emotional response at all was much more likely to fall flat.

A 2014 Facebook study on "emotional contagion" found that reducing the emotional content of users' feeds — either positive or negative emotion — led to those users posting less content to Facebook. Less emotion on Facebook, less posting on Facebook: that's a threat to the data feedback loop on which the company's business model relies.[4]

This was the environment that fake news — and, more broadly, hyperpartisan news — found so fertile. Some of the people creating those stories my hometown mayor shared were driven by their ideological commitments — but a larger number seemed to have been driven by money. If someone hits the right balance of anger and glee for a fake story to go viral, they can get millions of people to visit their website; throw on a few lines of code to put ads on it, and it can turn into a pretty decent payday. BuzzFeed reporters found a single town in Macedonia where hundreds of pro-Trump fake news sites were being run. ("In Macedonia the economy is very weak and teenagers are not allowed to work, so we need to find creative ways to make some money," one 17-year-old told them.)[5]

These sites, with names like the Denver Guardian and USADailyPolitics, were just close enough to real-sounding outlets and real-looking websites to be believable — at least within the environment of Facebook, where individual news brands are devalued compared with the platform experience. ("I saw it on Facebook" is the new "I read it in the Times.")

These sites also benefited from the social part of social media — the fact that their fake stories were often being distributed by very real people, like your friend or your mayor. Marketers have long known the power of word-of-mouth referrals and what psychologists call social proof. It isn't just some website telling you to read this story — it's someone you know.[6]

FAKE NEWS WEAPONIZES FILTER BUBBLES

Think of fake news as the trigger that weaponized social media's filter bubbles. When seeing an ideologically agreeable mix of news just meant reading more stories from National Review or The Nation, the boundaries of political discourse were still relatively narrow. But fake news, unbound by observed reality, colors issues of ideological gray into sharp black and white. Hillary Clinton was no longer a flawed candidate with a point of view you disagreed with; she was now someone who regularly murdered her political enemies. That's how algorithms helped conspiracy theories move from poorly Xeroxed newsletters to just another post on Facebook.

If you ask people whether they want an algorithm defining what news they see or hear, they tend to recoil. Instinctively, people don't like the idea of a computer determining which friend's baby photos are more important than which cousin's bon mots or which publisher's breaking news. One 2014 study found more than six in 10 Facebook users surveyed said they had no idea there was an algorithm determining their News Feed's order at all, and once informed, they weren't too happy about it.[7] A 2017 survey of more than 19,000 American adults found that 57 percent considered the algorithms used on platforms like Facebook and Twitter to select news stories "a major problem" for democracy.[8]

That Facebook study on "emotional contagion" I mentioned earlier? The main hypothesis it tested was whether or not the company could cause, by manipulating the News Feeds of more than 600,000 of its users, those people to be markedly more happy or sad. (It turns out they could! Shading the News Feed in one direction or the other for just a few days led users' own posts to take on the same emotional color.) When those findings were revealed in a dry academic paper, the blowback was enormous. Many users had not fully internalized the constructed nature of their Facebook experience or the degree to which re-weighting a few variables in an algorithm could impact their actual emotional state.

Instagram's shift to algorithmic ordering in 2016 and Twitter's dalliance with the same both led to huge user protest. (#RIPTwitter was the hashtagged heart of the rebellion.)[9] But in both cases, the platforms reported that their embrace of algorithms had led to significantly greater engagement from users. And, of course, there's been no mass retreat from Facebook, which now has more than 2 billion regular users.

The reality remains that the amount of information available to be consumed — on Facebook or any other successful social platform — does nothing but increase. And while laid-off journalists may wish Mark Zuckerberg would hire them all to recreate newspaper Page 1 meetings, there simply doesn't appear to be a realistic way to consistently judge editorial quality at a scale of 2 billion users. Facebook already employs many thousands of people to monitor content in the areas where it is legally required to (hate speech, violence, pornography). Those decisions can be complex in nature, but they're still easier to make than verifying whether or not John Podesta held a Satanic dinner or if there are any FBI agents who've mysteriously turned up dead.

In the aftermath of the 2016 election, Facebook did begin to collaborate with a number of independent fact-checking organizations to identify dubious stories and — if they're found to be false by at least two different organizations — flag them as "disputed" for users. But that effort has had little impact; Facebook has revealed few details about its efficacy, but an employee from one of the fact-checking outfits told a Bloomberg reporter that only about 100 stories a month were being debunked. Needless to say, that's barely a ripple in an ocean.[10]

And even if Facebook were to somehow commit to a massive global verification effort — a Full Employment Act for fact-checkers — that would raise at least as many questions as it answers. Facebook already has huge power over so many corners of our lives — do we really want them determining capital-T Truth too? And any attempt at a solution that might work in the United States or Europe would also need to make sense in the context of nations with weaker democracies or far lesser press freedom — places where government complaints of "Fake news!" have real teeth.

THE GOOD AND BAD OF ALGORITHMS

Unless someone finds an off switch for the internet, it seems likely that algorithms will continue to drive an increasing portion of the news we receive. So it's useful to identify some of the ways they can harm or improve the information ecosystem.

The potential for trouble heightens whenever the incentives of a platform's business model run in opposite directions to the stated aims of the algorithms they build. For example, Facebook has an overarching interest in keeping its users within the Facebook world, and it has been willing to use its algorithms to encourage that. When Facebook wanted to increase the amount of video uploaded to and watched on its service, its largest roadblock was the runaway success of Google's YouTube. So it made Facebook-uploaded video look more appealing in the News Feed than YouTube videos — with a much larger thumbnail, better presentation of accompanying text and autoplay, which meant that merely scrolling by a video would start it playing without sound.

That preferred presentation — and the inflated metrics created by autoplay and an exceedingly generous definition of what counts as a video "view" — made it clear to publishers that they had to be uploading directly to Facebook to get video traction there. In short order, Facebook had used the News Feed's power — specifically its power to make whatever Facebook likes more appealing than what it doesn't — to make itself a worthy rival to YouTube.

Facebook did much the same to publishers when it introduced Instant Articles in 2015. The pitch: Hey, publishers. Your websites are slow and janky, and you're terrible at selling ads on smartphones. We know how run servers and sell ads! Why don't you publish those stories of yours directly within Facebook? We'll sell the ads and take a 30 percent cut of the revenue.

It was a well-timed pitch in many ways. Publishers, watching their audiences move to mobile devices, were struggling to make their websites load quickly on slower mobile networks and the display ads they sold for desktop browsers were ineffective on phones. They were already seeing the digital advertising market be eaten by Facebook and Google; if you can't beat 'em, maybe it's time to join 'em?

On the other hand, creating a superior reading experience inside Facebook would seem to hand further power to the company that was eating publishers' audiences. Publishing to Instant Articles required reallocating some of news organizations' already lean technical resources. And Facebook's constraints meant some of publishers' most compelling work, like data visualizations and interactives, just wouldn't work.

Major publishers, for the most part, signed on. But by early 2017, many had cut back deeply or walked away from Instant Articles entirely, including The New York Times and The Guardian, finding that whatever revenue gained wasn't worth the loss of audience control and the risk to subscription products. But it was only the latest example of major news organizations changing their editorial and business strategies in response to the whims of Facebook.

Another important factor is the degree to which an algorithm allows tiny amounts of data — even a single user action — to alter the information it then feeds back to users. If you've ever searched for something unusual on YouTube, you may have seen how responsive the video platform's recommendation engine can be to just a single piece of information. (One evening of curiosity can leave you with Cajun accordion video recommendations for weeks.)

In 2017, a BuzzFeed reporter started a completely fresh Facebook account — with no click history and no friends — and liked a few mainstream Republican pages. When Facebook suggested more pages to like, he liked them. Other than that initial seeding with mainstream Republicans, all the other data Facebook had about this new user was based on actions Facebook itself had recommended to him. Within minutes, his News Feed began to fill up with conservative memes; within hours, the fake news started rolling in (chemicals being dumped in the water supply to turn people gay); within four days, he was seeing white power memes, posts promoting Russian President Vladimir Putin and neo-Nazi propaganda. In a statement, Facebook noted, accurately, that an account without any friends is not the standard use of Facebook. But the exercise showed how quickly mainstream ideas can be supplanted by radical ones in the News Feed.[11]

Other social platforms can optimize even more quickly. Mike Caulfield of Washington State University Vancouver has demonstrated that on Pinterest a new account can, simply by pinning two images and visiting two web pages, be turned into a den of anti-vaccine and other health-related propaganda.[12] Twitter's trending topics are a frequent vector for conspiracies and false information and have been shown to be open to manipulation by bot networks and tight influencer collectives. Instagram is a big area of growth for misinformation, too.[13]

ALGORITHM TIPS FOR NEWS CONSUMERS

If a social platform is interested in being a better citizen when it comes to civically useful news and information, it should do a better job of making its algorithmic actions transparent to the user.

If a feed is recommending something unexpected, a user should be able to find out what, exactly, led to that recommendation.

Ideally, a platform should allow users to tailor how its algorithms work. Do you want a ton of news or no news at all? Want to go heavy or light on memes? Filter out all the neo-Nazis and trolls, or keep them all in? Mute all Yankees fans for the summer or amplify them? There are a ton of reasons why users might want to change the feed a platform delivers them, either permanently or temporarily, and companies should do a better job of serving them.

In the meantime, the responsibility to navigate these systems will continue to rest primarily with users — many of whom have little of the media and digital literacy needed to do so.

1. Be aware of how a platform's choices might be tied to your previous actions. Use whatever tools the platform does offer to curate your feeds; blocking and muting tend to be the most powerful.

2. If you think your likes and comments aren't generating the content you want, be more aggressive about liking and commenting on the content you do.

3. Many platforms allow you to delete some or all of the past data that's been collected on you, even if they don't make it easy — take advantage.

On the other hand, maybe the hassles of fake news, disinformation and public blowback will be sufficient for some platforms to voluntarily check out of the news game. In January 2018, Facebook announced a major change to its core algorithm: Posts from publishers and other companies would be significantly de-emphasized in the News Feed, replaced with more content posted by friends and family. In the announcement, Mosseri called it an effort to "bring people closer together and build relationships." Zuckerberg said that reading news is too often "just a passive experience" and that there would now be less news in people's feeds. The algorithm will now judge articles based on the degree to which they encourage "meaningful interactions between people" — a concept that still seems to be defined by those quantifiable likes, comments and shares.

Perhaps that will serve as a final admission that evaluating comment threads is easier than determining capital-T Truth. But a cynic might note that Facebook will still offer a solution for publishers and companies seeking a way back into the News Feed. It's called buying an ad, and it's how Facebook makes about 98 percent of its revenue.

CHAPTER SIX

Beliefs Versus Facts: Getting The Brain To Change Its Mind

By Jonas T. Kaplan

Beliefs Versus Facts: Getting The Brain To Change Its Mind

onsider the following question: Why do firefighters who score higher on measures of risk-taking perform better on long-term measures of career success? Perhaps it's because firefighting is inherently risky; surely if one is prone to avoiding danger, this isn't the wisest career choice, as appealing as the thought of sliding down that pole and driving a big red truck with flashing lights at high speed may be. Clearly, to be a great firefighter one has to be willing to charge into a burning house without hesitation.

There's just one problem with this explanation. It isn't actually true that risk-taking firefighters are better at their jobs. The piece of information that I snuck into my first sentence was bogus. Hogwash. Malarkey. Fake news. It was made up by social psychologists Craig Anderson, Mark Lepper and Lee Ross for an experiment they conducted on Stanford undergraduates in 1980. Some of the students were told, as you were, that risk-taking firefighters are more successful. But others were told the exact opposite: it's conservativism that correlates with success. No matter which way the relationship was described, students believed it, and what's more, even after being told that the information was made up, they still believed whatever they were initially told. This study and many more like it have confirmed that like a few extra pounds around the waist, beliefs are much easier to put on than they are to take off.

This resistance we have to revising our beliefs once they are formed can pose a problem. Part of what makes life better now — compared to a thousand years ago — is the tremendous amount of new knowledge that humankind has accumulated. Our models of the world have grown in sophistication and utility, as we have replaced, reformed and rejected old views about reality in favor of newer, better ones. But our unwillingness to revise our beliefs frequently gets in the way of important progress. Consider the well-publicized case of anti-vaccination beliefs. In 2014 an investigation by the Hollywood Reporter found that vaccination rates at schools on the west side of Los Angeles were lower than in many developing African nations. This situation is a textbook case of belief fixation: Many parents persist in believing a thoroughly discredited relationship between autism and vaccination. As in the Stanford experiment, merely delivering information about the safety of vaccines doesn't seem to help either. In some cases anti-vaccine beliefs seem to grow even stronger when challenged, a phenomenon known as the "backfire effect."

However, unbridled credulity brings its own dangers. In fact, we should always be skeptical of new information. In addition to the deluge of false news and conspiracy theories on the internet, we live in a world of ubiquitous advertising, bombarded by messages expertly crafted to persuade us. If we simply believe everything we encounter, we will end up wearing magnets on our wrists to improve our health and sending money to Nigeria in hopes of claiming our inheritances.

Tasked with walking this line between stubbornness and gullibility is the human brain, an organ that has spent the vast majority of its existence concerned with keeping us alive in the wilderness — guiding us away from snakes and bears, making sure we don't eat poisonous plants and encouraging us to take care of those immediately around us. Relative to the billions of years that it took life to develop the world's most sophisticated mechanism for keeping an organism alive, it is mere decades that we have applied it to the job of avoiding email scams while simultaneously keeping an open mind with regards to medical knowledge about vaccines.

So in the quest to understand the psychology of belief, we must look to our biology. The brain is three pounds of flesh and blood, and its primary concerns, keeping the organism and its immediate kin safe and alive, inform everything it does. When we think about some of the most sophisticated things the brain does, like creating and understanding language, producing art and music, or devising formulae that describe the physics of the universe, it's easy to get carried away with the metaphor of the brain as a computer, coldly calculating information encoded in electrical spikes instead of ones and zeros. The brain is processing information, but it is doing so in consultation with a warm body. While neuroscience has a long way to go in understanding how the brain accomplishes these complex tasks, recent neuroimaging research has supported the ideas that our most sophisticated reasoning abilities are still grounded in our most ancient biology, and that what we believe is tied to who and what the brain considers worth protecting.

INSTINCTS FROM THE GUT

If we conceive of the brain as the steward of a living body, then we should start by understanding how it knows what to do. One of the most important nerves that brings information about the internal organs to the brain is called the vagus nerve, which comes from the Latin word for wanderer (think vagrant or vagabond), because it wanders throughout the body and makes contact with many of the visceral organs. Carrying information from all of these organs in the viscera, the vagus enters the brain from below, where its reports are first read by some of the oldest parts of the brain, in the brainstem. From there information travels upward, notably making a pit stop in a structure known as the insula. The insula (Latin for island), is a little island of very old cortex nestled right between the more modern frontal and temporal lobes (see Figure 1). This communication between the brain and the internal organs of the body is, of course, a two-way street, with signals from the brain traveling back down to the body, forming complex feedback loops and allowing for a kind of conversation.

The insula is an interface between the old and the new — in addition to its downward connections with the brainstem, it is also connected with some of the most modern parts of the brain in the prefrontal cortex that help us with some of our most complex plans and decisions, and form the basis of our personalities. In its role as an integrator of information from the body, the insula helps to generate many of our "gut feelings," and its connections with the cerebral cortex facilitate the incorporation of these feelings — essentially sensations from the body, information about what the body is doing — into our more complex cognitive processes and decision-making strategies. For instance, we all may have felt our heart racing when we think about an upcoming consequential decision, or

> *"Nature is a tinkerer, not an inventor."*

we might feel "butterflies in our stomach" before a significant event. So the term "gut feelings" is a metaphor grounded in reality. One feeling the insula seems to be particularly important for is the feeling of disgust. When we encounter something the nervous system really does not want us to ingest, we have a strong negative feeling that encourages us to avoid it. We feel sickened or nauseous and we recoil away from the source of our disgust. For example, you might feel this when you see rancid meat. I feel it when someone puts ketchup on a hot dog.

The French biologist Francois Jacob famously said that nature is a tinkerer, not an inventor. When a new problem comes along in evolution, instead of inventing a new solution out of whole cloth, life uses what it has. Since the brain has this very old, very effective system for turning us away from things that it deems unhealthy, this valuable tool doesn't only get pulled out of the toolbox when it comes to food. It also gets leveraged to solve other, similar problems. One of those similar problems relates to our firmly held beliefs.

WATCHING THE BRAIN CHANGE ITS MIND
ABOUT POLITICAL BELIEFS

In a recent study that my colleagues Sarah Gimbel, Sam Harris and I conducted at the Brain and Creativity Institute,[1] we wanted to know what happens in the brain when we are confronted with evidence that contradicts our cherished beliefs. Because we were interested in what happens when people resist changing their minds, we started with a population and a set of beliefs we knew would be hard to change — political beliefs. For this study, we recruited people who described themselves as committed liberals and we identified a set of political beliefs that all of these people claimed to hold very strongly, things like "taxes on the wealthy should be increased" and "the war on terror has been an ineffective response to the attacks of Sept. 11." We also found a set of beliefs that our participants claimed to hold just as strongly, but weren't political in nature, such as "Thomas Edison invented the light bulb" or "fluoride helps prevent tooth decay."

We then put them inside a functional MRI scanner so that we could measure their brain activity as they read arguments and evidence against these strongly held beliefs. fMRI is a technology that uses principles of magnetic resonance imaging to track transient changes in blood oxygenation. This allows us to infer where changes in neural firing are taking place. Once inside the scanner, we presented them with challenges to their beliefs. For example, we told them about Humphry Davy's demonstration of an electric lamp to the Royal Society 70 years before Edison, or how Edison's patent on the electric light bulb was invalidated by the U.S. Patent Office, which found that it was based on the work of another inventor. After they read these counterarguments, we asked them again to tell us how strong their belief was (they rated their belief on a scale from 1 to 7 where 1 is totally disbelieve and 7 is strongly believe), so we could see to what degree, if any, we had changed their minds.

As expected, we found that it was easier to change people's minds on some topics than on others. For example, poor Thomas Edison's status was easily dismantled, but beliefs about abortion and gay marriage didn't budge.

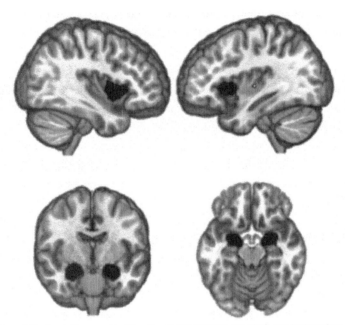

Figure 1: The insula (top row, black) and amygdala (bottom row, black, two brain regions concerned with emotion and feeling, found to correlate with resistance to belief change.

Predictably, political beliefs were considerably less flexible than non-political beliefs for our participants. We also found that some people were more flexible than others. When we looked at all the different people who participated in our study and compared them based on how much they changed their minds, we noticed something interesting: Individuals who were most resistant to changing their minds were the people who showed the most brain activity in the insula while being challenged.

So the insular cortex, a brain region first concerned with monitoring the internal state of the body, doing things like notifying us when we are about to eat rancid meat, is now helping us to make decisions not only about what kind of food to ingest, but also about what kind of information to ingest.

This finding connects our struggle with sifting through information to our deeply rooted biology. Signals that are processed through this route are often attributed to intuition, our less conscious form of reasoning that depends heavily on feelings from the body. To emphasize the role of intuition in belief and persuasion, the psychologist Jonathan Haidt has used the metaphor of an elephant and a rider, where the conscious, rational rider struggles to direct the large, lumbering, automatic and emotional elephant.[2] The activity we are measuring in the insula may be a reflection of the reins in this metaphor, pulling between the elephant and the rider as they interact to produce a direction. Another recent study found that the insular cortex was particularly active when people considered beliefs that are "nontestable"[3] — those beliefs we have that aren't directly based on evidence. In our previous work we have also found the insula to increase in activity when people consider religious beliefs compared with nonreligious beliefs.[4] These are the kinds of beliefs where we tend to rely most on our intuitive, gut feelings.

In addition to the insular cortex, we also looked at another brain region known to be important for emotion, the amygdala. It is a small, almond-shaped region buried deep in the anterior part of the temporal lobe that is important for detecting emotionally salient stimuli in the environment, particularly things that pose a threat to us. The amygdala helps us to notice when there is something out there we should be cautious of, whether it is a spider or a person who might not be worthy of our trust. People with damage to their amygdalae tend to be overly trusting of others. In our study, this brain region also showed increased activity in response to challenging information in people who were less likely to change their minds, suggesting that the amygdala plays a role in wariness toward information as well as people.

This research reminds us that separating emotion from cognition is artificial. We aren't computers, we are living organisms. How we feel is always intertwined with how we think and how we decide. And it should be — it's part of the intelligence of the body that life itself has given us through its billions of years of trial and error. That said, there are many caveats in interpreting this kind of research.

First, we must be cautious with the temptation to conclude that because a given brain region was active, we therefore know what was happening psychologically, a process known as "reverse inference." Because each brain region participates in multiple tasks, and we don't fully understand them yet, there are always alternative explanations. For instance, one emerging conception of the anterior insula is that it is involved in the detection of salience, a role that is more attentional than purely emotional. Meanwhile, one recent study on the neural basis of belief revision found that the insula was specifically engaged when people detected that a belief needed to be revised, and interpreted the insula's role as alerting them that revision was required.[5] These explanations aren't necessarily incompatible, but of course we should always be open to having our beliefs on the matter revised.

Other cautions relate to the specific design of our experiment. First, we only tested people with liberal political beliefs. There is reason to believe that some of the brain structures described here might function differently in conservatives. The amygdala has been found to be physically larger in conservatives, and conservatives also may activate the insula more readily. Another important detail is that much of the challenging evidence we presented to subjects was, in fact, not completely true. In order to present the most compelling counterarguments, we used statements that contained exaggerations and distortions of the truth. To the extent that our subjects had expertise on the issues we probed, they may have been reasonably suspicious of many of the counterarguments. And while that skepticism is part and parcel of the process we intended to study, and gives our experiment a resonance with the real-world situations we encounter so frequently on the internet these days, without further research it is difficult to say how it affects the results.

WHO THE BRAIN THINKS WE ARE

The role of these emotional systems in protecting our beliefs shows us that the brain is interested in protecting more than just the physical body. The self it deems worthy of protecting also includes the contents of our minds — our beliefs, ideas and values. And this should really come as no

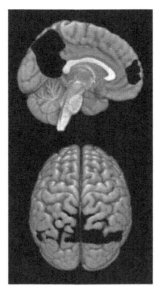

Figure 2: The brain's "Default Mode Network," views of the midline surface of the left hemisphere, and the whole brain from the top.

surprise. What we believe, particularly about important topics such as politics and religion, can be essential to how we define who we are. But rarely do beliefs thrive in isolation. Many of our strongest beliefs, including those that are political or religious, are shared among communities; they connect us to some people and separate us from others. And, it turns out, many of the other brain systems that play a role in belief maintenance are those that serve roles in thinking about who we are and who we are connected to.

Here's some background on how this works.

Functional brain imaging has traditionally been concerned with identifying regions of the brain that increase their activity during particular psychological tasks. Early neuroimaging studies tended to feature short stretches of a cognitive task interspersed with short periods of a blank screen or fixation cross, during which time subjects were asked to just rest quietly. These quiet, resting periods served as a baseline to compare with the active task. But in the late 1990s, neuroscientists began to ask just what exactly was happening during those "resting" periods. It turns out that there are several brain regions that seem to light up as soon as the lights go off. That is, these brain regions increase their activity levels when we aren't engaged in a specific, goal-directed task. The network was dubbed the "Default Mode Network" by neuroscientist Marcus Raichle, who used the name to suggest that the brain was returning to some default state when we aren't otherwise engaged.

Understanding what exactly this network does is an area of active research. In the last couple of decades, we've learned quite a bit about the Default Mode Network, or DMN. First, it is comprised of a set of highly interconnected hubs (see Figure 2). Two of these hubs (the medial prefrontal cortex, or MPFC, and the posterior medial cortices or PMC) are located along the midline of the brain — that is, the inner surfaces of the brain where the left and right hemispheres face each other. The other hubs are found on the lateral or outside surfaces of the parietal and temporal lobes. The second important thing that we've learned is that while it is true that the DMN decreases in activity during most goal-directed tasks, and turns on when we ask people to simply rest, there are in fact specific cognitive processes that activate it. When asked to rest, the mind does not truly lie idle. It is in this wide-open space that our mind is free to wander, to daydream, to leave the here and now and travel to other places and times, to think freely.

One type of thinking that seems to activate these brain structures is social cognition: thinking about people and relationships, thoughts and intentions. This finding has led some to theorize that our brains "default" to a mode of thinking that is inherently social. And certainly when left to our devices as in the resting state, we spend a lot of time thinking about people we know and what they are up to. A related activity that engages the DMN is thinking about one's autobiographical self. The autobiographical self is the aspect of yourself that mentally extends into the past and future, forming a story of who you have been and where you are headed: your recollections of childhood, your reasons for choosing your career, your ideas about the kind of person you believe yourself to be. For example, one common experimental paradigm that has been found to activate the MPFC and PMC is one where you are asked to decide if various personal traits describe you. Are you an honest person? Are you impatient? Are you friendly? When answering questions about one's self, the brain's midline structures tend to become more engaged.

As you may have guessed, the DMN, which seems concerned with self and social identity, is also activated when thinking about our deepest beliefs and values. In neuroimaging studies, we employ control conditions that allow us to make very specific inferences about what the brain is doing in our task of interest. For example, if you read a sentence that represents one of your beliefs inside an fMRI scanner, you are going to engage a wide array of brain regions that are involved in things like visual processing, reading, and understanding language. If we aren't interested in those processes, we try to make a comparison between two similar conditions that only differ in one important way. For example, in our study, if we take the brain activity recorded while you are reading arguments against your political beliefs and subtract the activation measured during nonpolitical beliefs, we'll leave aside anything that reflects reading or visual processing, and be left with brain regions that respond to whatever is special about political beliefs.

When people in our study read information that contradicted their po-litical beliefs compared with their nonpolitical beliefs, we found increased activity in all of the nodes of the DMN. There is also a similar pattern when people read stories expressing values that are deeply important to them, and when they are asked to make decisions about their religious, com-pared to nonreligious, beliefs. And while understanding of the DMN is still evolving, this pattern of results is consistent with the idea that part of the reason political beliefs are so resistant to change is that they touch core aspects of our social identities. An attack on our beliefs may be akin to an assault on the biological encoding of our very identity.

After all, consider what it is like to switch political parties. In the course of this research, I have been contacted by several people who told me about their experiences. At best, this change involves the straining of some person-al relationships, pushback from friends or cold shoulders from family and relatives. In extreme cases, it can require a complete rearrangement of the party-switcher's life and career. Beliefs do not exist apart from the rest of the mind; they are the beams and sometimes the foundation of a psychological home. Replacing them is no simple matter; in some cases, you may need to renovate the whole house. This is partly why older beliefs may be favored over new information: we have already built up around the old. Recall the example in the first paragraph about the firefighters: Once we think about why riskiness is associated with good firefighting, we now have more to excavate than just the original fact. We have a whole theory to reckon with.

WAYS NEWS CONSUMERS CAN TRAIN
THEIR BRAINS TO NAVIGATE FAKE NEWS

Despite the very real challenges of effectively navigating the informational maelstrom of modern life, our brains have our best interests at heart, and this can be helpful to remember when we feel our temperatures, our heart rate or our voices rising during a debate that might hit a little too close to home, challenging our core beliefs. What is objectively true might not matter much to a threatened brain that is tasked primarily with survival.

But while this may be discouraging at face value, there is a deeper glimmer of real hope to be found as well. Although belief challenge tends to be met with automatic resistance, the truth is that our lives are rarely in immediate danger during political disagreements. Rejection of new information, on the other hand, can result in very real harm. This suggests that shifting the way information is presented or how it is received to reduce the perception of personal threat is likely to be helpful in supporting productive political discourse.

Some research supports this strategy.

· There are indications that self-affirmation — exercises that let us feel a little better about ourselves — may buffer against the threatening effects of challenging information.[6] Feeling good about ourselves helps us to feel less threatened when challenging information arrives.

· It could be that simply understanding the role of feelings in processing new information will lead to more objective consumption of that information — a kind of mindfulness effect. Armed with knowledge about the role of our feelings in information processing, we may be able to consciously cushion ourselves against the feelings of defensiveness or fear that arise when we encounter new knowledge.

· We also may discover that becoming more expert at emotion regulation, which could have the added side effect of improved mental health, succeeds at leaving us more open to new information.

· Given the role of social binding and identity in belief maintenance, finding common social ground with those we are interacting with may aid successful communication.

· Most importantly, by framing questions about information processing in a way that acknowledges its biological basis, and by incorporating emotion and identity into our considerations, we may make our way to more and better answers.[7]

CHAPTER SEVEN

Correcting The Record

By Alexios Mantzarlis

Correcting The Record

2016 was a bumper year for political fact-checking. "Truth squading" of some variety has been a feature of American journalism for at least 30 years.[1] But it wasn't until the 2016 presidential election that fact-checking became a dominant format of political reporting.

To be clear, fact-checkers have had other moments in the national spotlight. During the 2004 vice presidential debate, then-Vice President Dick Cheney invited viewers to read Factcheck.org's articles on attacks made by his Democratic rival, John Edwards, concerning Halliburton, which Cheney headed before joining the Bush White House in 2001. (Cheney erroneously said the site's URL was Factcheck.com, which was quickly snatched up by a supporter of the Democratic ticket in an ironic confirmation of the importance of fact-checking.)[2]

Five years later, fact-checking was recognized with a Pulitzer Prize, awarded to PolitiFact in the National Reporting category. (Disclosure: PolitiFact is a project of the Poynter Institute-owned Tampa Bay Times.) The Pulitzer Board noted that the initiative "used probing reporters and the power of the World Wide Web to examine more than 750 political

Vice President Dick Cheney and John Edwards at the 2004 vice presidential debate.

claims, separating rhetoric from truth to enlighten voters."

In the 2012 presidential election cycle, Republican Mitt Romney's team had two major run-ins with fact-checkers.[3] First, GOP pollster Neil Newhouse disputed a correction by saying that "we're not going to let our campaign be dictated by fact-checkers." Later that year, during the second presidential debate, moderator Candy Crowley of CNN got into hot water for intervening imperfectly on a factual dispute that was less than black-and-white.[4]

These anecdotes notwithstanding, in its early years, the primary consumers of fact-checking articles were Beltway operatives and politics junkies. Even as recently as 2014, Americans expressed relatively low levels of familiarity with the fact-checking movement in journalism. (Somewhat inconsistently, the same YouGov survey found that the movement was viewed favorably by a vast majority of respondents.)[5]

But things changed in 2015. Both the demand for and supply of political fact-checking exploded.

To start with, each of the "Big Three" political fact-checking op-

Fact-checking Awareness and Attitudes

How familiar or unfamiliar are you with the fact-checking movement in journalism, which includes websites such as PolitiFact and Factcheck.org?

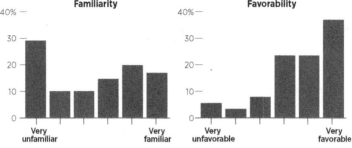

Source: YouGov survey conducted September 21-27, 2014.

erations — Factcheck.org, PolitiFact and The Washington Post's Fact Checker blog — broke online traffic records.

Factcheck.org's page views were up 148 percent in 2016 compared with 2012.[6] PolitiFact surpassed the 110 million page view mark in 2016, almost twice the traffic of the year before and a 133 percent increase from 2012, the year of the previous presidential election.[7] The Post's Fact Checker attracted a whopping six times more unique visitors in 2016 than it had in 2012 — and traffic kept growing in 2017 even though the election was over. (None of these projects have comparable traffic figures for 2008.)

And it wasn't just the "Big Three" that were fact-checking. The Duke Reporters' Lab found that 52 fact-checking initiatives were active across the country by Election Day 2016, up from 37 a year earlier.[8] New entries included local, national and international media organizations looking to cover the election in a way to which American voters seemed increasingly attuned.

Like the "Big Three" efforts, these projects also were of great interest to the U.S. public. NPR's live fact-checking of the presidential debates was its most popular digital project ever, drawing 7.4 million page views from 6 million users in only two days.[9]

Journalists also began citing fact-checking in their news reports. Whereas stories from the campaign trail would traditionally include

Bloomberg TV offered on-screen fact-checking for the 2016 presidential debates.

more-than-occasionally misleading talking points by candidates or their surrogates, political reporters started calling out blatant falsehoods after quoting them, often by referring their audience to fact checks published elsewhere.[10] During news shows, CNN corrected falsehoods on their chyron scrolls across the bottom of TV screens.[11] Bloomberg TV even provided some on-screen fact checks for the presidential debates.[12]

And yet.

If 2016 was the best year for truth-sleuthing in the digital age, it was also its worst year. A burst in fact-checking seems to have coincided with an epidemic of fact-twisting.

Republican candidate Trump repeatedly made false assertions, such as his claim that the real unemployment rate was 42 percent. The bogus internet-fueled "Pizzagate" conspiracy theory that Hillary Clinton was running a pedophilia ring from a Washington pizzeria led an armed man to terrorize the staff and patrons of Comet Ping Pong.[13] A BuzzFeed analysis found that the top fake news pages, containing deliberately false information, were reaching more people than the main stories from legitimate media outlets.[14]

This wasn't a purely American phenomenon, either. In Indonesia, the race for mayor of Jakarta was poisoned by a faked video purporting to show the Christian frontrunner making disparaging remarks about the Muslim majority.[15] In Italy, four of the 10 most shared stories on the constitutional referendum were entirely fabricated.[16]

2016: THE SO-CALLED "POST-TRUTH" YEAR

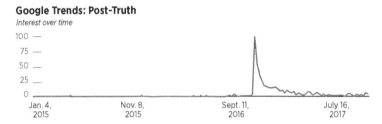

Google Trends: Post-Truth
Interest over time

Figure: Google Trends searches for "post-truth."

In the summer of 2016, headlines around the world started proclaiming the advent of a "post-fact" or "post-truth" era.[17] This culminated in the Oxford English Dictionaries selecting the latter as its "Word of the Year."[18]

Defined as "relating to or denoting circumstances in which objective facts are less influential in shaping public opinion than appeals to emotion and personal belief," the term hardly denotes a new phenomenon in politics. When droves of first-time voters voted for Barack Obama in 2008, were they doing so because of objective facts? Or were they moved by the more emotional campaign slogans of "Hope" and "Change?"

More broadly, "post-truth" has been used by liberal commentators to mean that voters — and especially Trump voters — are now so partisan that they flat-out reject any fact that contradicts their preferences.

The "post-truthers" usually make their cases based on anecdotal information. When they do choose to back up their thesis with research, it has often been by overselling the so-called "backfire effect" (see Chapter Four for a more detailed description). This was coined by political scientists

Brendan Nyhan and Jason Reifler in 2010, who detected that individuals holding misperceptions about the Iraq War appeared to double down on their false beliefs after being corrected.

This highly cited study, however, could not be replicated in the fall of 2016 when tested by Ethan Porter of George Washington University and Thomas Wood of Ohio State University.[19] Porter and Wood tried to detect the backfire effect by correcting 8,100 respondents on 16 different claims. Across the board, they found that while partisanship had an effect on the initial level of belief in a falsehood, it did not deter people from updating their understanding correctly after being fact-checked. In a heartening sign of good academic practice, Nyhan and Reifler partnered with Porter and Wood to conduct a new experiment — that found once again no sign of the backfire effect.[20]

In a similar study in France, researchers from the Paris School of Economics and Sciences Po found that fact-checking 2017 French presidential candidate Marine Le Pen's claims was equally effective in correcting voters' misperceptions.[21]

Overall, then, the evidence seems to suggest that people are fact-resistant, not fact-immune.

The demise of the backfire effect doesn't negate our other cognitive shortcomings, such as the confirmation bias and motivated reasoning. It is true that humans seek out information that conforms with their worldviews and tend to explain away facts that don't.

At the same time, it is not the case that people are so blinded by ignorance or partisanship that they don't pay attention when they are told that a lie is a lie.

A study published on the Royal Society Open Science journal found that Trump voters were less likely to believe four of his false claims after they were fact-checked (negating, once again, the backfire effect). What the study also found, however, was that voting preferences were unchanged. Trump voters were as likely to vote for their preferred candidate after being shown that his four statements were whoppers as they were before.[22]

This points to one of three major phenomena that collided to create today's unique context for facts in public discourse: Trump himself, whose

Belief in Trump and Unattributed Misinformation

Belief in Trump and unattributed misinformation and facts over time, across Trump support groups and source conditions.

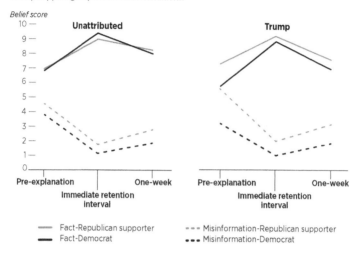

Belief in Trump and unattributed misinformation and facts over time, across Trump support groups and source conditions. Rep, Republican; misinfo, misinformation. Dotted lines show misinformation items.

penchant for falsehoods appears to be paradigmatically new in recent American history. Second, trust in the media and major party politicians is at historic lows, making it harder for facts to be believed. Finally, the major tech platforms we rely on to obtain information and interact with other citizens turned out to be dangerously permeable to misinformation campaigns.

Trump, trust and tech. We'll see precisely how each of these variables precipitated our current situation and what we can do moving forward.

TRUMP

When he announced his candidacy for the Republican presidential nomination in May 2015, Donald Trump was no stranger to fact-checkers.

During President Barack Obama's first term, he fanned the flames of the birther conspiracy, tweeting in August 2012 that "An 'extremely credible source' has called my office and told me that @BarackObama's birth certificate is a fraud."[23] (His later conduct on this particular falsehood exemplifies his capacity to say one thing followed by its complete opposite and not acknowledge or care about the contradiction. We'll get to that later.)

Trump the presidential candidate ran on the same playbook of conspiracy theories and falsehoods.

He claimed that "thousands and thousands of people were cheering" in Jersey City, New Jersey, as the Twin Towers were felled on Sept. 11 — an event that has been documented by no one else.[24] He retweeted a graphic falsely claiming that white homicide victims were predominantly killed by black shooters (81 percent, when the real figure is 16 percent).

By the end of 2015, the Big Three had declared him one-of-a-kind for the frequency and flagrancy of his inaccuracies.

"In the 12 years of FactCheck.org's existence, we've never seen his match," the website posted. Its editors noted that while they had never before chosen "a single claim or a single person" in their annual roundup of major falsehoods, they made an exception for "The King of Whoppers."[25]

PolitiFact struck a similar note, finding that the "only real contenders" for its annual Lie of the Year award were campaign statements by the GOP presidential candidate.[26] The Washington Post's Fact Checker editor Glenn Kessler included three Trump claims in a collection of the "biggest Pinocchios of 2015," writing that "most politicians drop a claim after it has been fact-checked as false. But Trump is unusual in that he always insists he is right, no matter how little evidence he has for his claim."[27]

These negative accolades didn't alter Trump's style nor reduce his appeal with voters. As he went from success in the primaries to victory in the general election, Trump's fact-twisting didn't seem to turn voters off.

It is hard to tell whether and how many of Trump's voters truly believed his falsehoods. Many may have determined that these were secondary to other factors influencing their voting decisions, such as their desire to see a conservative judge appointed to the Supreme Court seat left vacant by the death of Antonin Scalia.

On one hand, pollsters did find high levels of belief in various Trump conspiracy theories among his supporters. A Public Policy Polling survey found that almost six out of 10 believed Obama was not born in the United States.[28] In the summer of 2017, when asked by Morning Consult and Politico "who received the most votes from the general population in the 2016 presidential election?" 47 percent of sampled Republican voters replied "Donald Trump."[29] (Trump had tweeted shortly after the election that "I won the popular vote if you deduct the millions of people who voted illegally.")

Other evidence, however, points at greater factual awareness. In the study published by researchers at the Massachusetts Institute of Technology and the University of Western Australia mentioned above, U.S. voters were asked to rate their belief in a Trump falsehood before and after reading a fact check that disproved it.[30] The study found that voters across the political spectrum believed an incorrect statement by Trump less after it was fact-checked, including his supporters. What didn't change was their willingness to vote for him. Fact-checking seemed to change minds — but not votes.

Why? Again, in part this could be explained by other factors dictating voting intentions. Another explanation is that Trump's lying was taken as a signal. As Evan Davis writes in his book "Post Truth," Trump's falsehoods appeared to be an indication that he supported his electorate rather than that he believed in what he was saying. "Making bold, questionable, and sometimes plainly untrue claims ... was a more powerful way of showing his allegiance than simply saying 'I am on your side,' which anyone might choose to say in order to win votes."[31]

Trump also seems uniquely unfazed when corrected.

GOP primary rival Sen. Ted Cruz, corrected by moderator John Dickerson during an early primary debate about Supreme Court nominations, stumbled a bit as he tried to justify his assertion. Trump has displayed no such self-doubt.

Confronted about a tweet erroneously tying a protester at one of his rallies to ISIS by Chuck Todd in the spring of 2016, Trump batted the question away with, "What do I know, all I know is what's on the internet."[32]

During a debate, Clinton accused her opponent of saying that climate change was a hoax perpetrated by the Chinese, to which he responded, "I never said that." His 2012 tweet stating exactly that is still online.[33] As president, asked by ABC's David Muir whether it was dangerous to spread the debunked claim that 3 to 5 million undocumented immigrants voted in the election without evidence, he replied, "Not at all because many people feel the same way that I do." This attitude of treating evidence as secondary to the assertion has been at times adopted by other White House officials, including Press Secretary Sarah Huckabee Sanders. Pressed about a video the president retweeted allegedly showing a Muslim immigrant beating up a boy on crutches in the Netherlands, Sanders said, "Whether it is a real video, the threat is real."[34]

Politicians long before Trump have repeated false or misleading claims to drill them into public discourse and fire up supporters. Italy's Silvio Berlusconi, another media-obsessed businessman-cum-politician, campaigned in 2013 on the abolition of the property tax by repeatedly suggesting that Italy's rate of home ownership was far higher than those elsewhere in Europe. It was not,[35] but this served as a "factual" underpinning for his policy proposal. Berlusconi's goal was to make a misleading claim sound believable in order to justify his key campaign promise.

With Trump, believability matters less. During the campaign, he repeatedly claimed that unemployment figures provided by the Bureau of Labor Statistics were "totally phony" and "fake," variously claiming that the unemployment rate was 18 to 20 percent, 24 percent, 32 percent, 35 percent, 40 percent and 42 percent.[36] Yet once in office, he told then-Press Secretary Sean Spicer to inform reporters that "they may have been phony in the past, but it's very real now." During the campaign he also flipped on birtherism, calling a press conference in September 2016 to state that "Hillary Clinton and her campaign of 2008 started the birther controversy. I finished it. I finished it. You know what I mean. President Barack Obama was born in the United States, period."

These were not the only times Trump has been fluid with his beliefs. In March 2017 he tweeted, "How low has President Obama gone to tapp [sic] my phones during the very sacred election process." In May, in the span of

90 seconds, he performed an about-turn on the topic during an interview with Dickerson. Pressed by the journalist to prove the wiretapping claims, Trump responded, "I don't stand by anything. I just — you can take it the way you want. I think our side's been proven very strongly. And everybody's talking about it." He added, "I have my own opinions. You can have your own opinions," before abruptly ending the interview.[37]

Trump was inconsistent in his attitude toward fact-checkers, too. They were "scum" during a rally but he claimed to be "honored" that they found that he was right during one of the debates.[38]

The consequence of this cacophony of incoherent claims is often generic confusion about all public discourse. Analyzing the Trumpian tendency towards contradiction, philosopher Michael P. Lynch wrote in The New York Times that "its repeated use can dull our sensitivity to the value of truth itself."[39]

Trump's uniqueness was not so much the extent to which he played loose with facts, then, but how much he defied logic itself. As The New Republic's Jeet Heer wrote, the implication was that "his assertion of the moment is the only thing that counts."[40] Whether by design or because of his communication style, Trump ultimately sowed doubt not on specific facts that didn't match his narrative but on the overall capacity of facts to dispute strongly held but factually erroneous beliefs.

Trump's communication style didn't happen in a vacuum, however. It was deployed in and succeeded because of the low trust environment. Let's break that down further.

TRUST

Facts are by definition empirical things. They can be measured, detected or asserted to prove their existence. Still, in our everyday life, we trust that sources of facts have done their work rather than empirically re-evaluate everything we read, see and hear.

We don't ask for someone's passport when they tell us their name or

Trust Breakdown With Consumers

Great deal or fair amount of trust

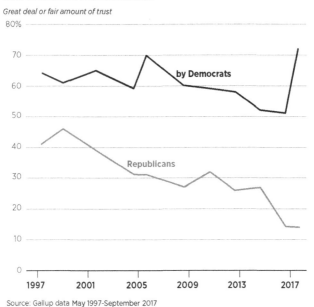

Source: Gallup data May 1997-September 2017

go to a lab to determine whether the store-bought water bottle actually contains H2O.

This same bond of trust ties media outlets to their audiences. Readers or viewers don't reach out to a story's sources to independently verify truthfulness. We have, generally speaking, accepted the truthfulness of what's reported unless proven otherwise.

That bond of trust is under severe stress. In 2016, Gallup found that only 32 percent of Americans trusted the media "a great deal" or "a fair amount" — the lowest figure on record.[41] On first glance it seems like the decline was reversed in 2017, with Gallup reporting a healthier 40 percent trust score. However, according to the Poynter Media Trust Survey,[42] the topline figure concealed a partisan divergence. While trust in the media spiked among Democrats (74 percent), it remained extremely low among Republicans (19 percent).

When that bond of trust breaks down, some news consumers may try to investigate things of their own accord — sometimes for good, sometimes with disastrous consequences, as was the case for Pizzagate's Edgar Welch — but most are probably just going to operate on the basis of constant cynicism about the news.

Even the best of media fact-checking can go only so far in this context. And what was on show in 2016 and 2017 has not always been the best fact-checking.

While many fact-checkers published timely and exhaustive work, there were plenty of shallow fact checks that targeted hyperbole, opinion or trivial claims. Outlets recognized that fact-checking was popular (and, in the case of Trump's most egregious claims, quite easy to conduct) and piled on with articles that were outright silly.

When Trump said that Clinton "acid washed" her servers, did we really need an NBC News fact check to say that this was false because actually she used a software called BleachBit? Or when Trump claimed that Obama "founded ISIS," did a nonsensical claim really need to be dignified with fact checks?

One of the key questions PolitiFact's staff asks itself before selecting a claim is "Would a typical person hear or read the statement and wonder: Is that true?" On several occasions editors across the industry hit "publish" on fact checks that did not meet this standard.

It wasn't just Trump, either. During a vice presidential debate, Politico felt the need to fact-check Democratic vice presidential nominee Tim Kaine's claim that "[Trump] loves dictators. He's got a personal Mount Rushmore: Vladimir Putin, Kim Jong-Un, Moammar Gadhafi and Saddam Hussein." If there was someone who genuinely believed that Trump had built a dictatorial Mount Rushmore in the back garden of his Mar-a-Lago property, then it's unlikely the fact check would sway them. To anyone looking for an excuse to not trust fact-checkers' findings on Trump, however, this allowed an out. See, they could tell themselves, fact-checking is a gimmick, not serious journalism.

Another issue was that as the Trump falsehoods piled up, stories about the frequency of incorrect statements — rather than the untruths themselves — became a subgenre of political coverage. New fact-checkers and old felt the need to crunch the numbers so they could say things like "Trump averaged about one falsehood every three minutes and 15 seconds over nearly five hours of remarks."[43] Highlighting the frequency of Trump's falsehoods isn't in itself a bad approach, but these collections often bundled together unlikely promises and hyperbole alongside lies. Again, this inconsistency would allow an effective motivated reasoner to discount the whole exercise as biased.

Imperfect samples also were presented as a form of social science. In December 2017, The New York Times compared Trump and Obama's misstatements. "In his first 10 months, Trump told nearly six times as many falsehoods as Obama did during his entire presidency." No effort was made to explain how the two presidents' statements were collected in a comparable manner.

This narrative then informed reactions to statements made by Trump and his advisers.

When Kellyanne Conway defended the White House's implausible claim that Trump's inauguration crowd was the largest in U.S. history by suggesting that the president had presented "alternative facts," a two-day news cycle ensued around the absurdity of the phrase. What was absurd, however, was the claim itself — not that objective evidence can never be contradicted by other evidence.

As I wrote for Poynter in January 2017, "Alternative facts do exist, though. That's why fact-checkers (usually) evaluate claims made by politicians on a scale rather than on a true/false basis. Whether a claim is true or not is determined by evidence that's more reliable and relevant to the claim at hand. Alternative facts may be irrelevant, but still true."

I agree with Davis when he writes in "Post-Truth" that turning the veracity of officials' statements into a battle for moral superiority isn't a good look for the media.

If the media goes down the path of believing that it must lead some special crusade in defence of truth, setting out each morning to take on the liars in positions of authority, it is likely to accentuate the sense of tribal rivalry and, if anything, exacerbate the tendency for opposing forces to spread falsehood.[44]

It's true that Trump has called the media names, settling on "fake news" as a catch-all for stories or news organizations he dislikes. But journalists should not fight back by positioning themselves as the rivals of the president's obfuscation rather than the advocates for the public interest. As soon as it becomes a question of us (Trump supporters) vs. them (the fact-checking media), there is no match to be had. According to one You-Gov poll from October 2016, a full 77 percent of Trump voters said they trusted media fact-checkers "not much" or "not at all."[45]

Sloppy fact-checking and shrill name-calling have proven counterproductive. Also counterproductive was a reticence to deploy fact-checking in a structured manner when it mattered the most: the presidential debates.

The Commission on Presidential Debates could be forgiven for being cautious about moderator fact-checking after the Crowley-Romney spat in 2012. But Commission President Janet Brown went far beyond caution when explaining her aversion to debate fact-checking to CNN's Brian Stelter.[46]

I think personally, if you start getting into fact-checking: what is a big fact, what is a little fact? And if you and I have different sources of information — does your source about the unemployment rate agree with my source? I don't think it's a good idea to get the moderator into essentially serving as the Encyclopaedia Britannica.

Brown's choice of examples was at the very least unfortunate, considering Trump's history with unemployment statistics. At a time of great debate over false equivalency in journalism, it also suggested that all facts were created equal when in fact there are higher-level sources for indicators as crucial to public policy as labor statistics.

Debate moderators, most notably NBC's Lester Holt and Fox News' Chris Wallace, did make a handful of on-the-fly corrections to the record.[47] But the lack of structured fact-checking matters because of the fragmentation of Americans' media consumption. The debates are probably the last piece of broadcast journalism that most politically curious Americans, regardless of political affiliation, see under exactly the same conditions.

If any opportunity for creating a shared reality existed, it was in this setting.

Possible interventions could have included dedicated air time for fact checks at the end of each segment or a final round of questions based on claims that fact-checkers have found to be false during the campaign.[48]

Alas, it wasn't to be, despite a majority of voters telling Monmouth University Polling Institute that moderators ought to "fact-check a candidate who states false information during the debate."[49]

Not fact-checking the debates represented such a missed opportunity because the fastest growing source of information for Americans — the internet[50] — turned out to be dangerously permeable to misinformation.

TECH

Just a few days after Trump won the presidential election, angsty liberal commentators started blaming his victory on fake news.

"Donald Trump Won Because of Facebook," was a typical headline, in this case from New York magazine. "The most obvious way in which Facebook enabled a Trump victory has been its inability (or refusal) to address the problem of hoax or fake news."[51]

However, no evidence has emerged since then to prove a clear-cut connection. In one study, published in January 2017, researchers at Stanford University determined that fake news articles would have had to be 35 times more effective than TV ads to have swayed the election.[52] Research published in January 2018 by the ubiquitous Nyhan with Reifler and Andrew Guess found that individuals who visited fake news sites often were also "voracious readers" of real news websites.[53]

This doesn't mean, however, that the new online information ecosystem hasn't had a role.

Facebook and Google's original mission statements promised a more connected world and a better information ecosystem. In many ways, that promise was not broken. The fact-checking boom described earlier would not have occurred without the access to information and audiences offered by the two platforms.

At the same time, however, both companies are first and foremost advertising behemoths. They understandably structure their services in order to maximize ad revenue. Because they are very good at it, click-based business models have proliferated. On Facebook, this led to false news with high engagement crowding out genuine news. In Google's case, this meant blogs denying that Obama was the first black president of the United States were highlighted in search results.

Both platforms have enacted policies to boost fact-checking. Facebook opened up a dashboard for fact-checking organizations it partners with to flag fake news stories. Google is highlighting fact checks so that users can see the rating of a claim directly in the search results.

But Google and Facebook didn't merely prove permeable to viral misinformation. They have also been very effective at providing fuel for our confirmation bias. As a study published in 2016 in the Journal of Computer-Mediated Communication found, frequent consumers of partisan news outlets are more likely to know what fact-checkers have concluded on a specific topic but less likely to agree with the conclusions.[54]

Possibly Facebook and Google's most disquieting effect, however, was to further reinforce the sense that there are many different truths and that it's well-nigh impossible to find an undisputed fact. This aligned with Trump's communication style.

Commenting on a viral tweet that falsely claimed paid protesters were being bused to a Trump rally, Lynch (the philosopher) wrote in The New York Times that "faced with so much conflicting information, many people are prone to think that everything is biased, everything conflicts, that there is no way to get out of the Library of Babel we find ourselves in, so why try?"[55]

The new online information ecosystem also exposed several weaknesses of the traditional fact-checking approach.

An intrinsic challenge is that a fact-check takes more time to be researched than a falsehood. "A lie can travel halfway around the world while the truth is putting on its shoes," says the popular aphorism, which is ironically often misattributed to Mark Twain. This rings even truer in the internet age. Leaked data from the Facebook fake news-flagging mechanism indicates that it can take "over three days" for a false news story to be fact-checked by its partners on the platform.

A second weakness was the selection process for fact-checked claims. Fact-checkers are typical high information media consumers, which is reflected in their selection of claims. Stories emerge from morning shows, talk shows, major institutional and campaign speeches and stories that are being covered by the mainstream media. But what was made starkly clear over the past few years is that there is a whole separate realm of public discourse entirely disconnected from these narratives. If you search for a breaking news event on Buzzsumo, a social monitoring service, you will notice that many of the stories with the highest engagement originate from alternative media outlets.

Finally, there is a question of formats. Misinformation travels in many formats, including memes and videos. Yet fact-checkers are still largely wedded to offering long, hyperlink-heavy chunks of text. That format works best as a repository of knowledge, but may not be the most effective counteragent to viral misinformation.

None of these obstacles is insurmountable. But it is the entire triad that defines today's information ecosystem — Trump, trust and tech — that must be addressed if we want facts to come out on top.

FACT-CHECKING FIT FOR 2020

Where do we go from here? Fact-checking went mainstream over the past two years. Yet its success hasn't translated into a more factual public discourse.

It is worth stressing, once again, that the situation is less dire than the catastrophists would have it. When they are asked, voters and audiences tend to support fact-checking, at least in principle. About 80 percent of survey respondents, for instance, told the Pew Research Center that they thought it was the media's role to fact-check political candidates and campaigns.[56]

Audiences didn't just turn up en masse for fact-checking over the past two years; they also pulled out their wallets to support the endeavor. The debunking website Snopes, facing a shutdown due to an ownership struggle in the summer of 2017, set out to pay its bills temporarily by asking its readers for help. It raised half a million dollars in 24 hours. PolitiFact's membership program, launched in January 2017, brought in more than $100,000 in its first few weeks.[57]

And we have seen that, generally speaking, those whose views are fact-checked mostly change their minds, at least in experimental settings.

With urgency but not unwarranted panic, therefore, here are some avenues we all can explore to give facts a fighting chance in the coming years.

For journalists:

Tone it down. Fact-checking should be about advocating for the truth, not conducting a crusade against lies. Shouting "liar," incessantly, getting worked up about hyperbole or extrapolating from nonscientific samples is counterproductive to ensuring that the truth matters.

Enlist fact-checkers of diverse backgrounds. Fact-checking is by definition agnostic of policy and nonpartisan. The raison d'être of many fact-checking projects is to ground political debate in a shared set of facts. However, different outlets can place a different emphasis on what is worth fact-checking — and be more likely to convince like-minded news consumers that a politician isn't saying the truth. As long as fact-checking is rigorous, transparent and accountable it can and should be launched within outlets of all editorial backgrounds.

Launch entirely new formats. Fact-checkers are experimenting with GIFs, short videos and other formats that go beyond the classic hyperlink-heavy, 1000-word article. As misinformation evolves, fact-checking must continue to evolve too.

Be consistent. CNN's chyron fact-checking got a lot of people excited in 2016, but was erratically deployed. If we introduce new formats to combat intentional falsehoods — and I am convinced that we should — then we ought to do so in a way that is consistently and transparently applied.

Reach out to skeptical readers. PolitiFact organized three community outreach events in cities that voted overwhelmingly for the president. (Trump voters, we have seen, expressed greater skepticism in fact-checking.) When they met them in person, critics found less to object to about fact-checkers than they did online. More academic efforts dedicated to learning about why specific misconceptions take hold are even more useful. A government-funded program is sending University of Georgia biologists to Burke County, Georgia, to help debunk local preoccupations about nuclear power. Lessons from that experiment should be followed closely by fact-checkers.

Show how the sausage is made. In proclaiming a victory for the "reality-based" media following Project Veritas' failed sting against The Washington Post in late 2017, columnist Margaret Sullivan wrote that "newspeople used to joke that readers should never be allowed to see how the sausage is made. Now we need to show that messy process as clearly as possible. Our very credibility depends on it." This is even more fundamental for fact-checkers, who are in the line of business of proving others wrong.

Change the incentive structure for accuracy on major platforms. Facebook and Google are moving towards changing the mechanisms by which information does well on their platforms. But more can be done, including helping publishers build an algorithmic reputation for accuracy and translate that into financial rewards, introducing genuine verification procedures that represent whether a publisher is committed to fact-checking and verification, providing nonemotional options for social media reactions and adding positive feedback loops in search engine and voice assistants based on the accuracy of the results found.

For media consumers:

Check your biases. If you are moved to share, retweet or forward a bombastic claim because it provokes an emotional reaction — take a beat. Remember that your decision affects your own audience of Twitter followers and Facebook friends. You probably apply some scrutiny to claims you find online that you find hardly believable; you should do the same with claims you really want to be true.

Read like a fact-checker. In a study co-authored by Sam Wineburg at Stanford University, fact-checkers were found to be far better at spotting fake news than Ph.D. historians. The simple skills they deployed — such as taking a look at the website before diving into the article, and repeatedly conducting deep searches to double-check key elements as they read — are effective ways for every reader to avoid getting fooled.[58]

Ask yourself "How do we know that?" Everyone is fallible, even fact-checkers. With skepticism but not cynicism we should always question a source of information. Was a dataset about sexual violence collected through surveys or through police reports? Different data collection methods may skew results in different ways — without making these false. Do the promoters of "Blue Monday" actually have a scientific way to determine which day is the most depressing of the year? Probably not.

Learn basic verification skills. Too many news consumers are digitally native but digitally naïve. Hoaxers use technology to produce false content — but fact-checkers also use it to debunk it. If you don't know how to use reverse image search to double check the origin of a picture, go learn how to right now. It's as easy as a right click, on some browsers.

And finally...

Keep measuring. For each of these efforts, we ought to try to measure success. Researchers should work with fact-checkers to see what formats, headlines and communication styles are more likely to lead partisans to change their view. Facebook and Google should share lessons from their efforts to combat misinformation with academics and news professionals thirsty for real-life data. News literacy campaigns should be evaluated for their capacity to inoculate students from fake news. And so on.

CHAPTER EIGHT

Russian Import Or Made In America?

Conspiracy Theories, Magical Thinking And State-Sponsored News

By Sarah Oates

Russian Import
Or Made In America?

Conspiracy Theories, Magical Thinking
And State-Sponsored News

Even in the aftermath of a presidential election that divided America, the specter of Russian propaganda influencing American voters has galvanized the attention of experts and citizens alike. While the U.S. audience has seemed relatively complacent about much of the propaganda and false information purporting to be news that appeared around the election, the idea that a foreign country is deliberately manipulating U.S. voters is one of the few concerns on which conservatives, liberals and those in between can agree.

But how much is Russia really the problem when it comes to deliberate fake news? Experts and observers have found plenty of troubling evidence of widespread fake news online that has nothing to do with Russia. This has led researchers to shift their focus from dismissing the circulation of conspiracy theories as merely sensational to considering it a central element in the U.S. media ecosystem. Evidence ranging from the Pizzagate violence caused by a fabricated story about a Hillary Clinton-backed pedophilia ring to the persistent belief among many Americans that former

President Barack Obama is a Muslim suggests that something is seriously awry in our information system.

The disturbing fact is that American citizens, especially those on the far right, have isolated themselves within alternative information "cocoons" that ignore traditional, fact-based journalism. This allows Russian disinformation to hide in plain sight in the U.S. digital media environment as people are both disengaged from reliable information sources and preyed on by political groups seeking to manipulate rather than to inform. Much of this is fueled by the shift in the audience's attention away from traditional media to "promoted" online news on social media platforms, especially Facebook. Facebook stands out as a game-changer in audience attention because its users can create trusted networks of like-minded friends and receive information tailored to their preferences by links promoted by friends, algorithms and advertisers.

There are three significant elements to consider in how Russia can surf the wave of fake news in America. First, researchers have been astonished by the persistent evidence of just how much Americans embrace a kind of "magical thinking," a belief in things that logic or even commonsense would dictate cannot be true. Second, it's important to measure how much pseudo-fact, rumors and outright lies are promoted or planted by groups in the fertile ground of the internet to deliberately mislead or fool American citizens. Finally, were the Russians just ahead of the curve by developing disinformation that was simultaneously misleading and entertaining? Is fake news a Russian innovation that has been exported to America?

AMERICANS AND MISINFORMATION

Researchers at the University of Washington set out to study "alternative narratives," or what people would generally call conspiracy theories, for mass shooting events. Kate Starbird and her research team analyzed tweets that were collected over a 10-month period, examining the tweeted

URLs to construct a map of how information was distributed across the web.[1] There were several shootings during the period analyzed, including at a nightclub in Orlando, Florida; in a shopping district in Munich, Germany; and at a mall in Burlington, Washington. Most of the tweets related to the nightclub shooting.

The researchers also read and analyzed the key websites that were mentioned, finding that online sources that promote "conspiracy theories and pseudo-science may function to conduct underlying political agendas." In other words, they are not simply making up stories; they are constructing elaborate narratives that reflect a general paranoia and distrust of the government.

Starbird and her fellow researchers found that conspiracy theories were by no means limited to obscure corners of the internet: Conspiracy theories appeared on websites that were defined as traditional news, clickbait, conspiracy/pseudo-science and places with marked political agendas. The tweets were a "collection of distinct alternative narratives that share several common features." In other words, it wasn't that a reader was perhaps believing that the one shooting may have been staged: Many readers were clearly buying into an entirely different worldview in which false flag, crisis actors and Zionist conspirators of "one narrative are combined with others in a mutually reinforcing manner."

This makes it easier to understand what happened at Comet Pizza in December 2016.[2] Edgar Welch had decided to come with a weapon to the Washington, D.C., restaurant to "self-investigate" a conspiracy theory that Clinton and her allies were running a pedophile ring out of the backrooms of the restaurant. On the face of it deeply absurd, this false narrative had been circulating in online forums and on conspiracy websites, part of the pervasive alternative universe of anti-state disinformation described by Starbird. But Welch wasn't alone in his conviction, which is based on no facts at all. A survey in the same month found that 46 percent of Donald Trump voters believed that leaked emails from the Clinton campaign talked about pedophilia and human trafficking. Even 17 percent of Clinton voters believed these baseless rumors.[3]

The problem is that Welch was not a "lone gunman." A lot of people have entered his self-reinforcing world of misinformation in which they have become unmoored from any sense of reality or reason as it has been understood in the United States. As other chapters in this book have emphasized, false information in the American media is nothing new. This has ranged from simple inaccuracies to lies deployed in the service of political interests, but research by Starbird suggests we have entered a new phase of magical thinking in which people have become completely detached from logic and firmly embedded in an "alternative" media universe in which facts are largely trumped by beliefs.

While Starbird herself reported she was shocked at the strength and extent of conspiracy theories in the United States,[4] other researchers point to the gap between perceived and desired reality. In other words, even when you can deploy information from established authorities to refute a conviction, people often don't care and, in fact, sometimes will cling to their beliefs all the more tenaciously if confronted with evidence that contradicts their worldview.[5] As a result, the more you try to show someone Obama's birth certificate, often the more they will cling to the idea that it is fake and that its existence is falsified.

This leaves journalists and politicians in a world in which traditional media norms — to give balanced and unbiased information to the public to develop strong citizens — often don't work. This has troubled researchers who believe that Americans should make political assessments based on fact. It is less mystifying if one considers that political decisions are often more visceral and emotional than rational. The problem, as demonstrated by Starbird and others, is that the ability to live in information bubbles in the online sphere exacerbates this tendency to an alarming degree.

According to a 2017 survey by the Pew Research Center, two-thirds of Americans get news from social media,[6] in particular by following suggested links to news stories. This means both self-selection into networks of like-minded individuals as well as algorithms that will reinforce news choice, partisan lines and — ultimately — reality constructed by information consumption.

Other research by Pew has highlighted an interesting difference in the media diet between the right and the left. A Pew survey in late 2016 found that 40 percent of Trump voters listed Fox as their main source of campaign news, more than all other sources combined.[7] On the other hand, barely any Clinton voters watched Fox — only 3 percent claimed it was their main campaign news source. More Clinton voters (18 percent) relied on CNN, but overall their media diet was more varied than that of Trump voters and included newspapers.

THE MALICIOUS USE OF MISINFORMATION

A critical question is whether the rise of magical thinking is a spontaneous outcome of the increase in digital information distribution or whether it has been encouraged by key political actors. There is compelling evidence that persistent false narratives are heavily promoted by political interests. Yet this cannot be explained as simply a group of teenagers in Moldova choosing to create fake news to earn money, a story that was widely covered during the 2016 elections. Instead, the malicious use of information is successful because of a synergistic relationship between those who effectively use the online sphere to attack political actors — and many right-wing U.S. citizens who use online media in a way that supports purveyors of disinformation.

Yochai Benkler and his colleagues at Data & Society studied 1.25 million stories published online between April 1, 2015, and Election Day 2016 (Nov. 8).[8] The researchers found a "right-wing media network anchored around Breitbart developed as a distinct and insulated media system." This "network" of linked websites broadcast a hyper-partisan view of the world with a pro-Trump agenda that "appears to have not only successfully set the agenda for the conservative media sphere, but also strongly influenced the broader media agenda, in particular coverage of Hillary Clinton." Separately, my own analysis of 2016 campaign news stories in The New York Times, The Washington Post and USA Today found that these mainstream media outlets gave a large amount of coverage to Trump-based scandals and rhetoric, but little to substantive issues. This meant that both rational discussion of issues and the Clinton campaign itself suffered as she had far more extensive policy expertise and experience than her Republican rival.[9]

Benkler et al. argue that the far-right media network created online was not fake news in the sense of "wholly fabricated falsities." Many of the most-shared stories in the network "can more accurately be understood as disinformation: the purposeful construction of true or partly true bits of information into a message that is, at its core, misleading." Benkler and his team highlighted some of the headlines, such as:

· The Anti-Trump Network: Fox News Money Flows Into Open Borders Group

· NY Times Bombshell Scoop: Fox News Colluded With Rubio to Give Amnesty to Illegal Aliens

· Google and Fox TV Invite Anti-Trump, Hitler-Citing, Muslim Advocate to Join Next GOP TV-Debate

· Fox, Google Pick 1994 Illegal Immigrant to Ask Question in Iowa GOP Debate

Americans are often irrational, but the partisan divide in the United States brings a new twist. The Economist/YouGov Poll from December 2016 found two interesting issues about conspiracy theories: a lot of Americans believe them and stubborn conviction plays out across partisan lines. This means that partisans are much less likely to believe news stories — whether widely demonstrated to be true or — if these narratives clash with their partisan interests. (Disclosure: The Economist owns CQ and Roll Call, which also use this polling with YouGov frequently.)

The poll also found that older conspiracy theories still held sway. For example, 36 percent of those surveyed still believed Obama was born in Kenya (despite Trump admitting that the then-president was born in the United States after years of publicly questioning the fact); 53 percent believed there were weapons of mass destruction in Iraq that the U.S. never found; and 31 percent still believed that vaccines have been shown to cause autism despite the complete discrediting of the flawed study that started the fake story. This suggests that the mainstream news media, which have extensively challenged these conspiracy theories, have limited ability to correct false convictions.[10]

Clinging to false assumptions is one thing. But when the same population holds opposing views on narratives, it suggests something has gone seriously wrong between the news media and audience. For example, 87 percent of Clinton voters in the survey reported that they believed that Russia hacked Democratic emails to help Trump, a story that has widespread evidence from a range of reputable media sources as well as government intelligence agencies. But only 20 percent of Trump voters reported that they believed the Russians had interfered on behalf of Trump.

Even winning an unlikely election isn't enough to convince many voters that some things aren't true. Despite no real evidence, 62 percent of Trump voters believed that millions of illegal votes were cast in the 2016 election, while even 25 percent of Clinton voters believed this as well. It seems that while the fog of false news promoted in the alt-right online network particularly reflects and fosters an alternative reality for Trump voters, disbelief and magical thinking have seeped into the mainstream as well.

RUSSIANS AND MISINFORMATION

While the research discussed above demonstrates that magical thinking and disinformation are not just a Russian export into the U.S. media system, it's still important to consider the intersection between Russian propaganda and conspiracy theories in the U.S. media. As outlined in other chapters in this book, the type and scope of the Russian information war in the 2016 U.S. elections is well documented. But what about the longer, deeper information war that Russia is waging against the United States? Russian propaganda outlets such as RT and Sputnik market themselves as traditional news outlets offering alternative news, attempting to construct narratives to resonate with what Russians perceive as disaffected Americans across the political spectrum. In addition, Russia has promoted these narratives through social media such as Facebook and Twitter.

The Russian actions in the United States are a manifestation of Russian media logic. Russia does not have a free media system and has increasingly limited freedom of expression online in recent years. Russians understand information as a political tool and use state-run media institutions, especially television, to promote narratives that support the Kremlin leaders. There are a handful of media outlets, including a weekly newspaper in Moscow, a Moscow radio station and some online news sources, that challenge the Kremlin line. Overall, though, media is understood as an extension of political power, as a way of manipulating public opinion rather than informing the public.[11]

> *"Russians have pioneered a style of disinformation called 'kompromat.'"*

While the Soviet system focused on predictable and persistent narratives such as the evils of the inequalities wrought by capitalism, the superiority of the "Soviet Man" and the constant attempts by the West to destroy the Soviet system, Russian propaganda has embraced more modern and compelling features. While anti-Western, pro-Russian narratives are still dominant, the Russians have pioneered a style of disinformation called "kompromat" (the abbreviation for 'compromising material' in Russian) in the post-Soviet era.

First used prominently in 1999 to attack a government official accusing Russian President Boris Yeltsin of corruption, kompromat is infotainment that can include video, accusations, half-truths and insinuations — often delivered by popular hosts of news analysis programs. A staple of kompromat is a sex video used to shame and embarrass rival politicians. In 2010, videos of Russian opposition journalists and politicians who had been filmed separately having sex with the same woman in a "honeypot" trap were leaked online. In 2016, an opposition political party was damaged

when a sex video of a married party leader and his aide was made public. Media manipulation and blackmail-by-media are certainly not the only weapons at the disposal of the Russian regime. The Kremlin has developed effective ways to systematically suppress opposition parties, control the legislature, interpret its constitution so that Putin is essentially president-for-life, use the court system to punish opponents and employ trumped-up charges to arrest, detain and imprison political opponents. However, media control and message management are key ways in which Russia's authoritarian regime keeps control over the population. In particular, the Russians have focused on media manipulation during elections so the disinformation deployed in the U.S. election is not surprising.

All of this means that Russia has been well positioned to take advantage of the modern digital sphere to pursue an information war against the West in general and the United States in particular. Americans either have a lot of catching up to do or need to figure out how to safeguard its media system from attack. The Kremlin has spent at least $1.5 billion between 2005 and 2016 expanding RT in foreign languages around the globe,[12] rebranding the former Russia Today television network into merely the initials RT with the slogan "Question More." RT claims that it is simply reframing news away from an Americentric point of view. However, as content analysis, statements by former employees and even a casual viewing of the channel show, RT news makes extensive use of disinformation and fake news as part of the Russian information war. For example, RT has repeatedly denied that Russian militants shot down Malaysia Airlines Flight 17 in 2014, killing all 298 aboard. The network has falsified information about Crimea and denied Russian military involvement in Eastern Ukraine — to name just a few of their departures from facts. The U.S. Justice Department required RT to register as a foreign agent in November 2017.[13]

There are two central points here. First, it is not only Russians who pursue foreign propaganda, as the United States also has Russian-language broadcasting in the former Soviet region. But content on U.S. government-funded outlets such as Voice of America and Radio Liberty must adhere to Western journalistic standards in their programming. While many vehemently disagree with American framing and interpretation of events, U.S. broadcasters in foreign countries do not employ the type of misinformation found on Russian media.

For those old enough to remember, there are echoes of Cold War propaganda in the lies and distortions on RT and other English-language news sources such as Sputnik from Russia. Indeed, the Soviet Union had a clear information policy that the role of the news media — at home and abroad — was to support the spread of Communism rather than to inform citizens. After the collapse of the Soviet Union in 1991, there was a great deal of chaos and challenge in the Russian media, but the role of the media as political player, instead of political watchdog, never shifted to a more Western liberal model.

INFORMATION WARFARE IN THE DIGITAL ERA

The digital world has given several important enhancements to post-Soviet propaganda. It is now easy to circumvent gatekeepers: Russians no longer need to work through Western intermediaries to disseminate information to American citizens. Indeed, social-media companies such as Facebook were happy to take advertising money from Russians to promote elements of the Kremlin's information war during the 2016 elections. While there are limitations in mainstream media on issues such as national security and pornography, there are de facto almost no controls on online content in the United States. This leads to the second advantage for the Russians in the current media environment. In an era of home-grown websites such as Breitbart and Infowars that thrive on magical thinking and conspiracy theories, Russian websites are not obviously foreign propaganda.

Nor is information warfare in the digital age a level playing field for all countries. The Russian government controls media content, in part through a series of laws that favor the needs of the government over rights of journalists and freedom of speech.[14] Online censorship and control, including by requiring all internet service providers operating in Russia to maintain information on users and content on servers on Russian soil, has accelerated in recent years and even months.[15] As a result, the United States (and other democracies) can't practice the same tactics on Russian citizens as the Russian government carries out on Americans. The Russian government has far greater control of both online and traditional media sources, as well as the ability to suppress any information that is not in the interest of the regime.

Here, the United States is constrained by the mismatch between its domestic media environment, which embraces information diversity and relies on the audience to sift through news, and countries that deploy aggressive propaganda. While the United States has dominated as a superpower in terms of military and economic might, it lags significantly in terms of information warfare. This leaves a critical opening for countries that oppose American domination and can exploit the vulnerabilities of an open media system with aggressive, state-sponsored disinformation campaigns aimed at U.S. citizens. These countries range from rogue states such as North Korea to powerful economic players such as China. Indeed, the question of China's influence was raised at the same congressional hearings that grilled U.S. social media companies about Russian propaganda. The New York Times reported that while there was no evidence of direct interference in the U.S. elections, China spends hundreds of thousands of dollars each quarter to advertise on Facebook, producing content in English that echoes Chinese propaganda themes about America.[16]

What does this all mean for the problem of conspiracy theories in the American media? The study by Benkler et al. as well as data from the Pew Center suggest that those on the far right in U.S. politics are likely to be simultaneously more interested in, and more vulnerable to, the narratives that the Russians tell about America. There is clear evidence that Russian propagandists make a deliberate attempt to echo far-right narratives and that Russian posting of pro-Trump information online was more likely to be shared on social media. For example, if you look at a sample of Russian-funded Facebook ads released during congressional hearings in 2017, the metrics from Facebook show that pro-Trump/far-right posts were likely to get more shares than Russian-sponsored posts targeted at the left.[17]

"Russian propagandists make a deliberate attempt to echo far-right narratives."

Evidence from Facebook and other social-media companies show that Russian posts also included appeals to liberal causes, such as the Black Lives Matter movement. Stephen Wilson's research found that the Russian strategy was to try to motivate protestors from the right and left out on to the streets, although evidence suggests that only one Russian social-media campaign actually managed to get people to organize a small Black Lives Matter demonstration.[18] Wilson found much of the efforts awkward and amateur, including websites simply copied and pasted into new URLs and language on social media clearly not written by native English speakers.

So what is the point of Russia posting on both the left and right? While there could be logic to supporting one candidate over the other — such as

Russian hackers deliberately targeting the Clinton campaign — it would seem somewhat nonsensical to insert Russian-sponsored messages for groups as divergent as Muslim-Americans and anti-immigrant supporters. The reasons remain unclear, although one conclusion would be that the Russians were merely testing the waters of disinformation in the American media digital sphere. At the same time, they undermined trust in the U.S. electoral system, the online network of news and — by extension — the media itself. Given that the media is a crucial factor in democracy and a constant threat to authoritarian states such as Russia, there is value in undermining public trust in the news media.

A WAKE-UP CALL

The Russian disinformation campaign in the U.S. in 2016 was successful in attacking American values and democracy through a divisive presidential election, but not really because of Russian strategy. Rather, the Russians exploited democratic challenges that the United States developed through its own political and media system. Trump has consistently used a Russian approach to the media, perceiving it as a tool to manipulate rather than to inform. He routinely broadcasts false information and denigrates the role of the media as a watchdog to inform the public. His administration, like that of Putin, is working to undermine freedom of the media on many fronts, in particular by recent changes that gives asymmetric power to large media owners by eliminating rules of media concentration.[19] The end of net neutrality in the United States signals an ominous shift of power away from equal access to the online sphere.

Media were critical in creating powerful political brands for both Putin and Trump. In the case of Russia, this was through the orchestration of media control in a society with little experience of a free press.

In the United States, the media too often prioritized style over substance and gave vast amounts of attention to outrage over Trump's constant attacks on women, minorities, political opponents and established political norms. The coverage, augmented by disinformation, magical thinking and conspiracy theory in the far-right online news network, has created powerful information bubbles that remain deeply resistant to normal news. Russia played the game a bit with its own media contributions, through RT and attempts at social media manipulation — but the game is dominated by American players.

What can we make of the specific Russian attempts to manipulate news? They only work in what Andrew Chadwick would call the "hybrid media system,"[20] in which traditional media amplify stories rooted in the online sphere. So it is most effective when the Russians can produce at least some smoking guns to influence news in reputable media outlets in the United States. The release of Clinton-related emails in the final moments of the 2016 campaign, considered to have been engineered by Russian hackers, was an example of this type of influence. The more overt, clumsy attempts at influence, such as by spoofing a black activist website, buying social-media ads to promote extremist views and trying to arrange real-life meetings from fake social-media accounts, are less attempts to change hearts and minds — but arguably successful demonstrations of the hollow nature of social-media communication. And Russia has a great interest in destroying trust in the internet, as the online sphere has a documented ability to empower citizens and mobilize resistance against authoritarianism.

But the problem isn't so much what Putin wants to do to the American media, it is how U.S. political leaders are using tactics that are more appropriate for an authoritarian state than for a democracy. In this case, media are used to create a fearful, confused population that no longer cares to distinguish fact from fiction. At its extreme, people rely on charismatic leaders to allay their fears, ceding the control of policies to elites who will rule in their own interests instead of for the common good.

It is not inevitable that foreign powers and bad actors can exploit the relative openness and commercial nature of the American media system to spread propaganda. But the example of Russian information warfare during the 2016 elections is evidence that a free media system is vulnerable to attack.

At this moment, there remains the danger that the U.S. media system can be used as a tool in support of the elites, as opposed to an instrument to inform the masses in a democracy. The extent of belief in conspiracy theories, particularly on the right, shows that the system is broken. And social media companies such as Facebook and Twitter have been slow to take responsibility for their role in the problem.

Ultimately, Russia may have given Americans an important gift. The revelations about Russian media manipulation may have served as a useful wake-up call for media policy and media literacy alike in the United States.

CHAPTER NINE

Final Thoughts

By Ellen Shearer

Final Thoughts

O n Jan. 17, 2018, Washington Post readers found a call to action
from Sen. John McCain on the op-ed page. But the senior senator from Arizona was aiming that call mainly at one reader: "Mr.
President," the headline read, "stop attacking the press."[1]

His attacks have "provided cover for repressive regimes to follow suit,"
McCain wrote. "The phrase 'fake news' — granted legitimacy by an American president — is being used by autocrats to silence reporters, undermine
political opponents, stave off media scrutiny and mislead citizens."

He ended with, "Only truth and transparency can guarantee freedom."

Mid-morning on the same day, McCain's fellow Arizona Republican
senator, Jeff Flake, delivered a speech on the Senate floor on the same topic
as McCain — "truth, and a principled fidelity to truth and to shared facts."

"2017 was a year which saw the truth — objective, empirical, evidence-based truth — more battered and abused than any other in the
history of our country." He laid the blame on Trump and his White House
for calling journalists "the enemy of the people" and creating the idea of
"alternative facts."[2]

Sen. John McCain

"It is the press's obligation to uncover the truth about power," he said. "It is the people's right to criticize their government. And it is our job to take it."

> *"It is the press's obligation to uncover the truth about power."*

Meanwhile, a Gallup/Knight Foundation survey of 19,000 Americans was released, showing that a majority of Americans worry about the effects of the spread of false information on democracy.[3]

That evening, Trump took to his favorite medium, Twitter, to fulfill his promise to present a new set of awards to the news media — for "fake news." He tweeted a link to find the list of "Highly-Anticipated 2017 Fake News Awards." The link, to the Republican National Committee, froze and offered only error messages for about the first hour.

"The most disturbing element was the spectacle of a sitting president orchestrating another attack on the news media," wrote Paul Farhi of The Washington Post,[4] which was named for one award for a tweet underestimating the crowd size at a Trump rally, by using an erroneous photo; it was quickly corrected.

Of the 10 awards, eight were for stories that were corrected — and resulted in the departures of two reporters — and two for tweets that were corrected.

Coincidentally, Flake had addressed journalistic mistakes in his speech: "A major difference between politicians and the free press is that the press usually corrects itself when it gets something wrong. Politicians don't."

Rising partisanship and dropping faith in nearly all institutions — Congress, the president, the federal government and certainly the news media — is a fact of 21st-century life so far. But combating the rise of false information from partisan or phony news sites, in particular, is relatively new — and so are Americans' worries about this phenomenon.

The Gallup/Knight Foundation survey found that 73 percent of Americans consider inaccurate information being spread on the internet a major concern in news coverage — a higher percentage than are concerned about any other potential type of news bias.

"A majority of U.S. adults consider 'fake news' a very serious threat to our democracy," the report noted.

However, about 40 percent of Republicans think accurate news that reflects badly on a politician or party is fake news while Americans generally define fake news as knowingly portraying false information as true.

Americans also think the impact of social media — and politicians' use of it — has been negative at the same time that, the study said, equal proportions of people rely on social media as rely on newspapers to stay informed.

Only half are confident that there are enough news sources to allow them to cut through bias to sort out the facts. Even more disturbing, only 27 percent are "very confident" they can tell when a news sources is providing factual news versus opinion.

Twitter, not necessarily a factual news source but an information distributor certainly, demonstrated why there's reason not to be confident.

It sent a message to about 680,000 users that they had either retweeted, liked or followed a tweet from a Russian troll farm known as the Internet Research Agency during the 2016 election, as noted in

Chapter Two. It also said it has identified about 13,500 more Russian troll accounts being used during the election, bringing the total to more than 50,000.

Twitter also shared its plans for the 2018 midterm elections. It plans to verify that major party candidates' Twitter accounts are real and use anti-spam technology against bots and trolls.[5]

That same day, Facebook — which has been cited as the platform most used for spreading misinformation, as has been noted in earlier chapters — followed up on its announcement that it would be encouraging "more meaningful connections" and less public content, including news. Facebook plans to ensure that the news users do *"A nation that is afraid to let its people judge the truth and falsehood in an open market is a nation that is afraid of its people."* see is "high quality," said Adam Mosseri, head of Facebook's News Feed.[6]

"Starting next week," he wrote, "we will begin tests in the first area: to prioritize news from publications that the community rates as trustworthy" based on a survey of a diverse group of U.S. Facebook users to determine which news sources they are familiar with and trust.

"We'll be working on these efforts for the rest of the year. For the first change in the US next week, publications deemed trustworthy by people using Facebook may see an increase in their distribution. Publications that do not score highly as trusted by the community may see a decrease."

This is an interesting step that may, indeed, help people sort out truth from falsehood in online news.

But as this book has pointed out in each chapter, there are many other issues that news consumers should take into account: the effect of their own biases, the effect of algorithms on what they see, the "bad actors" deliberately trying to circumvent roadblocks such as the recent Facebook announcement, the need to be skeptical of information that confirms preconceptions, and more.

This book lays out some clear guideposts to help you on the journey to finding the news most close to the truth.

To quote President John Kennedy: "A nation that is afraid to let its people judge the truth and falsehood in an open market is a nation that is afraid of its people."[7]

Notes

CHAPTER 1

1. Steven R. Weisman, *Daniel Patrick Moynihan: A Portrait in Letters of an American Visionary* (New York: Public Affairs, 2010). Weisman references the interview that invoked the famous quote.

2. Charles Sykes, "Does the Truth Matter? This Is No Longer a Theoretical Question," *America*, June 5, 2017.

3. As of 2016, Gallup's report on America's trust in mass media showcased a sharp drop during the course of the election. The poll was conducted by phone Sept. 7–11, 2016, with a random sample of 1,020 adults and a margin of error of plus or minus 4 percentage points.

4. Johnnie L. Roberts wrote for Newsweek in 2006 about the loss of nightly news audiences. See Roberts, "The Future of Evening News," *Newsweek*, April 16, 2006.

5. Matthew Ingram, for *Fortune*, reported in 2017 that while the digital advertising industry continues to grow, smaller companies are unable to compete with the two largest players: Google and Facebook. See Ingram, "How Google and Facebook Have Taken Over the Digital Ad Industry," *Fortune*, Jan. 4, 2017.

6. American Press Institute and AP NORC Center for Public Affairs Research, "Who Shared It? How Americans Decide What News to Trust on Social Media," 2017.

7. In one case, stories might have been generated by the Russians. A lab called the Internet Research Agency generated 470 Facebook pages and purchased 3,000 ads with those profiles during the time leading up to the election.

8. Researchers at Indiana University in Bloomington studied how fake news is systematically spread. See "First Evidence That Social Bots Play a Major Role in Spreading Fake News," *MIT Technology Review*, Aug. 7, 2017.

9. Garry Kasparov's wise words, quoted from his tweet of Dec. 13, 2016, resonated with those reeling from the results of the year's election.

10. Brian Resnick, writing for *Vox*, dove into multiple examples of the "illusory truth effect" and why our minds allow us to believe things simply with constant repetition. See Resnick, "The Science Behind Why Fake News Is So Hard to Wipe Out," *Vox*, Oct. 31, 2017.

11. The Trusting News project helps journalists take responsibility in the fight against misinformation. See https://trustingnews.org/.

12. Moderators are hesitant to check candidates during debates. See Callum Borchers, "To Fact-Check or Not to Fact-Check? That Is the Moderators' Question," *Washington Post*, Sept. 23, 2016.

13. Mark Zuckerberg posted a 6,000-word manifesto about the company's global ambitions in February 2017.

14. David Shedden, "Today in Media History: In 1947, the Press Reported on the Hutchins Commission Report," Poynter Institute, March 27, 2015.

CHAPTER 2

1. Sam Levin, "Facebook and Google Promote Politicized Fake News About Las Vegas Shooter," *Guardian*, Oct. 2, 2017.

2. Joshua Gillin, "Rats! Rumors of Rat Meat Passed Off as Chicken Wings Are Fake News," *PolitiFact*, March 6, 2017.

3. Nicholas Confessore and Daisuke Wakabayashi, "How Russia Harvested American Rage to Reshape U.S. Politics," *New York Times*, Oct. 9, 2017.

4. See Donald Trump's Twitter post of Feb. 17, 2017.

5. Pepe Escobar, "Hillary, Queen of War: The Road Map Ahead," *Sputnik*, Aug. 4, 2016.

6. Michael Barthel, Amy Mitchell and Jesse Holcomb, "Many Americans Believe Fake News Is Sowing Confusion," Pew Research Center, Dec. 15, 2016. The telephone survey of 1,002 U.S. adults was conducted Dec. 1–4, 2016, with a margin of error of plus or minus 3.6 percentage points.

7. Joy Mayer, "Who Trusts — and Pays For — the News?" Reynolds Journalism Institute, July 27, 2017.

8. See also Sami Main, "These Are the Most and Least Trusted Brands in News," *Adweek*, Aug. 7, 2017.

9. Adam Mosseri, "Working to Stop Misinformation and False News," Facebook news release, April 6, 2017.

10. Sam Wineburg and Sarah McGrew, "Lateral Reading: Reading Less and Learning More When Evaluating Digital Information," Stanford History Education Group Working Paper No. 2017-A1, Oct. 6, 2017.

11. Hunt Allcott and Matthew Gentzkow, "Social Media and Fake News in the 2016 Election," *Journal of Economic Perspectives* 31, no. 2 (2017).

CHAPTER 3

1. "A Lesson in Fake News From the Info-Wars of Ancient Rome," *Financial Times*, Jan. 17, 2017.

2. Leonard W. Doob, "Goebbels' Principles of Propaganda," in *Public Opinion and Propaganda: A Book of Readings* (New York: Dryden Press, 1954).

3. Steve Coll, "Donald Trump's 'Fake News' Tactics," *New Yorker*, Dec. 11, 2017.

4. Jaclyn Reiss, "Trump Again Publicly Tells CNN's Acosta: 'You're Fake News,'" *Boston Globe*, Aug. 14, 2017.

5. Rosie Gray, "Trump Defends White-Nationalist Protesters: 'Some

Very Fine People on Both Sides," *Atlantic*, Aug. 15, 2017.

6. "Trump Shuts Down CNN Reporter," CNN, Jan. 11, 2017.

7. "'You Are Fake News!' Trump Refuses to Let CNN Reporter Ask Question," Fox News, Jan. 11, 2017.

8. Julie Vitkovskaya, "Breaking Down the Trump Dossier: What You Need to Know," *Washington Post*, Oct. 26, 2017.

9. Jack Shafer, "Trump's Fake Jihad Against the Fake News," *Politico*, Oct. 17, 2017.

10. Carol E. Lee, Kristen Welker, Stephanie Ruhle and Dafna Linzer, "Tillerson's Fury at Trump Required an Intervention From Pence," NBC News, Oct. 4, 2017.

11. Harriet Sinclair, "Rex Tillerson Still Won't Deny He Called Trump a Moron," *Newsweek*, Oct. 15, 2017.

12. Maggie Haberman, Glenn Thrush and Peter Baker, "Inside Trump's Hour-By-Hour Battle for Self-Preservation," *New York Times*, Dec. 9, 2017.

13. Trump delivered remarks at the FBI National Academy graduation ceremony on Dec. 15, 2017.

14. Twitter user shannon4t76, for example, retweeted the Conservative Stamp story on Dec. 14, 2017, adding, "You better be doing a VERY detailed investigation @JohnHMerrill - as an AL citizen I am watching this closely. 2018 election is coming quickly."

15. Kim LaCapria, "Did Roy Moore Receive 953 Votes to Doug Jones' 5,327 in a Town of 1,867 Registered Voters?" Snopes, Dec. 15, 2017.

16. Joshua Gillin, "If You're Fooled By Fake News, This Man Probably Wrote It," *PolitiFact*, May 31, 2017.

17. The online poll, conducted Oct. 12–16, surveyed 1,991 registered voters, with a margin of error of plus or minus 2 percentage points. See Steven Shepard, "Poll: 46 Percent Think Media Make Up Stories About Trump," *Politico*, Oct. 18, 2017.

18. Brian Stelter, "Three Journalists Leaving CNN After Retracted Article," CNN, June 27, 2017.

19. Vivian Wang, "ABC Suspends Reporter Brian Ross Over Erroneous Report About Trump," *New York Times*, Dec. 2, 2017.

20. "ABC News Statement On Michael Flynn Report," ABC News, Dec. 2, 2017.

21. Nancy Gibbs, "A Note to Our Readers," *Time*, Jan. 24, 2017.

22. Julia Manchester, "Washington Post reporter apologizes for tweet on crowd size at Trump rally," *The Hill*, Dec. 9, 2017.

23. Manu Raju and Jeremy Herb, "Email Pointed Trump Campaign To Wikileaks Documents," CNN, Dec. 8, 2017.

24. Abby Phillip and Mike DeBonis, "Without Evidence, Trump Tells Lawmakers 3 Million to 5 Million Illegal Ballots Cost Him the Popular Vote," *Washington Post*, Jan. 23, 2017.

25. Maggie Haberman and Jonathan Martin, "Trump Once Said the 'Access Hollywood' Tape Was Real. Now He's Not Sure," *New York Times*, Nov. 28, 2017.

26. Jason Schwartz, "Trump's 'Fake News' Mantra a Hit With Despots," *Politico*, Dec. 8. 2017.

27. Paul Dallison, "David Cameron to Trump: Your 'Fake News' Act Is 'Dangerous,'" *Politico*, Dec. 13, 2017.

28. Saphora Smith, "British PM May Issues Rare Rebuke of Trump for Retweeting Anti-Muslim Videos," NBC News, Nov. 29, 2017.

29. Channel 4 News, "The White House Responds After Trump Retweets Three Anti-Muslim Videos," Twitter, Nov. 29, 2017, 9:54 a.m, https://twitter.com/Channel4News/status/935929948963033088.

30. Chloe Farand, "Reports Syrian Regime Hanged 13,000 Prisoners Branded 'Fake News' by Bashar al-Assad," *Independent*, Feb. 10, 2017.

31. Samantha Schmidt, "Trump Chuckled as Duterte Called Journalists 'Spies.' That's No Joke in the Philippines," *Washington Post*, Nov. 14, 2017.

32. Jason Schwartz, "Trump's 'Fake News' Mantra a Hit With Despots," *Politico*, Dec. 8, 2017.

33. John McCain, Twitter, Dec. 13, 2017, 12:27 p.m., https://twitter.com/SenJohnMcCain/status/941041856661598209.

34. Eugene Scott, "Mccain: Dictators 'Get Started By Suppressing Free

Press,'" CNN, Feb. 20, 2017.

35. Kim LaCapria, "Snopes' Field Guide to Fake News Sites and Hoax Purveyors," Snopes, Dec. 8, 2017.

CHAPTER 4

1. Michael Shermer, *Why People Believe Weird Things* (New York: W. H. Freeman, 1997).

2. Daniel Kahneman, *Thinking, Fast and Slow* (New York: Farrar, Straus and Giroux, 2011).

3. Shermer, *The Moral Arc* (New York: Henry Holt, 2015).

4. White House Office of the Press Secretary, "Remarks by President Obama in Address to the People of Europe," Hannover, Germany, April 25, 2016.

5. See Johan Norberg, *Progress: Ten Reasons to Look Forward to the Future* (London: OneWorld Publications, 2016); Peter Diamandis and Steven Kotler, *Abundance: The Future is Better Than You Think* (New York: Free Press, 2012); Matt Ridley, *The Rational Optimist: How Prosperity Evolves* (New York: Harper, 2011); Steven Pinker, *The Better Angels of Our Nature* (New York: Penguin, 2011); Gregory Clark, *A Farewell to Alms: A Brief Economic History* (Princeton, NJ: Princeton University Press, 2007).

6. Shermer, *Heavens on Earth* (New York: Henry Holt, 2018).

7. Roy Baumeister, Ellen Bratslavsky, Catrin Finkenauer, and Kathleen D. Vohs, "Bad Is Stronger Than Good," *Review of General Psychology* 5(4): 323-370.

8. Richard Thaler, Daniel Kahneman, and Jack Knetsch, "Experimental Tests of the Endowment Effect and the Coase Theorem," *Journal of Political Economy* 98, no. 6 (Dec. 1990).

9. Curry Kirkpatrick, "Cool Warmup for Jimbo," *Sports Illustrated*, April 28, 1975.

10. Opening scene of *The Armstrong Lie*, directed by Alex Gibney (2013).

11. Pinker, *Enlightenment Now: The Case for Reason, Science, Humanism,*

and Progress (New York: Viking, 2018).

12. Mark Snyder, "Seek and Ye Shall Find: Testing Hypotheses About Other People," in *Social Cognition: The Ontario Symposium on Personality and Social Psychology*, ed. E. T. Higgins, C. P. Heiman and M. P. Zanna (Hillsdale, NJ: Erlbaum, 1981).

13. John M. Darley and Paul H. Gross, "A Hypothesis-Confirming Bias in Labelling Effects," *Journal of Personality and Social Psychology* 44 (1983).

14. Shermer, *The Believing Brain* (New York: Henry Holt, 2011).

15. Drew Westen, Pavel Blagov, Keith Harenski, Clint Kilts and Stephan Hamann, "The Neural Basis of Motivated Reasoning: An fMRI Study of Emotional Constraints on Political Judgment During the US Presidential Election of 2004," *Journal of Cognitive Neuroscience* 18 (2006).

16. Jonathan Haidt, *The Righteous Mind: Why Good People Are Divided by Politics and Religion* (New York: Random House, 2012).

17. Resolution of Heterodox Academy, heterodoxacademy.org.

18. The USA Today/Gallup poll was conducted by telephone May 3–6, 2012, with a random sample of 1,024 U.S. adults. The margin of error was plus or minus 4 percentage points.

19. See Shermer, "The Liberals' War on Science," *Scientific American*, Feb. 1, 2013.

20. Alex B. Berezow and Hank Campbell, *Science Left Behind: Feel-Good Fallacies and the Rise of the Anti-Scientific Left* (New York: Public Affairs, 2012).

21. Lecture given at a conference on science and skepticism at the University of California, San Diego, August 2017.

22. Dan M. Kahan, Kathleen Hall Jamieson, Asheley R. Landrum and Kenneth Winneg, "Culturally Antagonistic Memes and the Zika Virus," *Journal of Risk Research* (2017).

23. Leon Festinger, Henry W. Riecken and Stanley Schachter, *When Prophecy Fails: A Social and Psychological Study* (New York: Harper-Collins, 1964), 83.

24. Carol Tavris and Elliot Aronson, *Mistakes Were Made (But Not by Me)* (New York: Houghton Mifflin, 2007).

25. Brendan Nyhan and Jason Reifler, "When Corrections Fail: The Persistence of Political Misperceptions," *Political Behavior* 32, no. 2 (2010).

26. Personal correspondence with Tavris, October 2016.

CHAPTER 5

1. Adam Mosseri, "From F8: How News Feed Works," Facebook, April 22, 2016.

2. E. Bakshy, I. Rosenn, C. Marlow and L. Adamic, "The Role of Social Networks in Information Diffusion," *Proceedings of the 21st International Conference on World Wide Web* (2012), 519-528.

3. James B. Stewart, "Facebook Has 50 Minutes of Your Time Each Day. It Wants More," *New York Times*, May 5, 2016.

4. A.D. Kramer, J.E. Guillory and J.T Hancock, "Experimental Evidence of Massive-Scale Emotional Contagion Through Social Networks," *Proceedings of the National Academy of Sciences* 111, no. 24 (2014), 8788–8790.

5. Craig Silverman and Lawrence Alexander, "How Teens in The Balkans Are Duping Trump Supporters With Fake News," *BuzzFeed*, Nov. 3, 2016.

6. Naveen Amblee and Tung Bui, "Harnessing the Influence of Social Proof in Online Shopping: The Effect of Electronic Word of Mouth on Sales of Digital Microproducts," *International Journal of Electronic Commerce* 16, no. 2 (2011), 91-114.

7. M. Eslami, A. Rickman, K. Vaccaro, A. Aleyasen, A. Vuong, K. Karahalios, K. Hamilton and C. Sandvig, "I Always Assumed That I Wasn't Really That Close to [Her]: Reasoning About Invisible Algorithms In News Feeds," *Proceedings of the 33rd Annual ACM Conference on Human Factors in Computing Systems* (2015) 153-162.

8. "American Views: Trust, Media, and Democracy," Knight Foundation, Jan. 16, 2018. The Gallup/Knight Foundation survey was conducted by mail.

9. Alex Hern, "Jack Dorsey Calms #RIPTwitter With Carefully Worded Non-Denial," *Guardian*, Feb. 8, 2016.

10. Sarah Frier, "Facebook Stumbles With Early Effort to Stamp Out Fake News," *Bloomberg*, Oct. 30, 2017.

11. Ryan Broderick, "I Made A Facebook Profile, Started Liking Right-Wing Pages, and Radicalized My News Feed in Four Days," *BuzzFeed*, March 8, 2017.

12. Mike Caulfield, "Digital Polarization on Pinterest," YouTube video, Nov. 13, 2017.

13. Jonathan Albright, "Instagram, Meme Seeding, and the Truth about Facebook Manipulation, Pt. 1," Berkman Klein Center, Nov. 8, 2017.

CHAPTER 6

1. J. Kaplan, S. Gimbel and S. Harris, "Neural Correlates of Maintaining One's Political Beliefs in the Face of Counterevidence," *Scientific Reports* 6 (2016).

2. Jonathan Haidt, *The Happiness Hypothesis* (New York: Basic Books, 2006).

3. Jonathon Howlett and Martin Paulus, "The Neural Basis of Testable and Non-Testable Beliefs," *PLOS One* 10 (2015).

4. S. Harris, J. Kaplan, A. Curiel, S. Bookheimer, M. Iacoboni and M. Cohen, "The Neural Correlates of Religious and Nonreligious Belief," *PLOS One* 4 (2009).

5. K. Lavigne, P. Metzak and T. Woodward, "Functional Brain Networks Underlying Detection and Integration of Disconfirmatory Evidence," *NeuroImage* 112 (2015), 138–151.

6. David K. Sherman and Geoffrey L. Cohen, "Accepting Threatening Information: Self-Affirmation and the Reduction of Defensive Biases," *Current Directions in Psychological Science* 11, no. 4 (2002).

7. For further reading, see *The Neural Basis of Human Belief Systems*, edited by F. Krueger and J. Grafman (Psychology Press, 2012).

CHAPTER 7

1. Lucas Graves, *Deciding What's True: the Rise of Political Fact-Checking Movement in American Journalism* (New York: Columbia University Press, 2016), 57.

2. Nick Anderson, ".com or .org? Cheney Suffers Slip of the Suffix," *Los Angeles Times*, Oct. 7, 2004.

3. Ben Smith, "Romney Camp Bets on Welfare Attack," *BuzzFeed*, Aug. 28, 2012.

4. Erik Wemple, "Did Crowley Fairly Fact-Check Romney? A Textual Analysis," *Washington Post*, Oct. 17, 2012.

5. Brendan Nyhan and Jason Reifler, "Estimating Fact-Checking's Effects: Evidence From a Long-Term Experiment During Campaign 2014," American Press Institute, April 28, 2015.

6. Email interview with the author.

7. Aaron Sharockman, "The Power of Fact-Checking in Today's World," *PolitiFact*, June 13, 2017.

8. Bill Adair, "Keep On Fact-Checking!" *New York Times*, Nov. 8, 2016.

9. Benjamin Mullin, "NPR's Real-Time Fact-Checking Drew Millions of Readers," Poynter Institute, Sept. 27, 2016.

10. Adair, "It's Time To Fact-Check All The News," Poynter Institute, Aug. 15, 2016.

11. Alexios Mantzarlis, "Why CNN's Fact-Checking Chyron Is a Big Deal — And Why It Isn't," Poynter Institute, June 3, 2016.

12. Mark Stencel of the Duke Reporters' Lab tweeted screenshots of Bloomberg TV's live fact-checking on Sept. 26, 2016, at 7:25 p.m.

13. Marc Fisher, John Woodrow Cox and Peter Hermann, "Pizzagate: From Rumor, to Hashtag, to Gunfire in D.C.," *Washington Post*, Dec. 6, 2016.

14. Craig Silverman, "This Analysis Shows How Viral Fake Election News Stories Outperformed Real News on Facebook," *BuzzFeed*, Nov. 16, 2016.

15. Yenni Kwok, "Where Memes Could Kill: Indonesia's Worsening Problem of Fake News," *Time*, Jan. 6, 2017.

16. "La notizia più condivisa sul referendum? È una bufala," *Pagella Politica*, Dec. 2, 2016.

17. See the author's Twitter thread of June 28, 2016, at 11:02 a.m.

18. "Word of the Year 2016 Is ..." Oxford English Dictionaries, 2016.

19. Mantzarlis, "Fact-Checking Doesn't 'Backfire,' New Study Suggests," Poynter Institute, Nov. 2, 2016.

20. Nyhan, "Fact-Checking Can Change Views? We Rate That as Mostly True," *New York Times*, Nov. 5, 2016.

21. Mantzarlis, "French and American Voters Seem to Respond in a Similar Way to Fact-Checking," Poynter Institute, May 5, 2017.

22. Mantzarlis, "Fact-Checking Changes Minds but Not Votes, According to New Research," Poynter Institute, March 1, 2017.

23. Donald Trump, Twitter post on Aug. 6, 2012, at 1:23 p.m.

24. Glenn Kessler, "Trump's Outrageous Claim That 'Thousands' of New Jersey Muslims Celebrated the 9/11 Attacks," *Washington Post*, Nov. 22, 2015.

25. "The 'King of Whoppers': Donald Trump," FactCheck.org, Dec. 21, 2015.

26. Angie Drobnic Holan and Linda Qiu, "2015 Lie of the Year: The Campaign Misstatements of Donald Trump," *PolitiFact*, Dec. 21, 2015.

27. Kessler, "The Biggest Pinocchios of 2015," *Washington Post*, Dec. 14, 2015.

28. Tom Jensen, "GOP Quickly Unifies Around Trump; Clinton Still Has Modest Lead," Public Policy Polling, May 10, 2016.

29. The Morning Consult/Politico online poll was conducted July 20–24, 2017, with a sample of 3,981 voters. The margin of error was plus or minus 2 percentage points.

30. B. Swire, A. Berinsky, S. Lewandowsky and U. Ecker, "Processing Political Misinformation: Comprehending the Trump Phenomenon," *Royal Society Open Science* 4, no.3 (March 1, 2017).

31. Evan Davis, *Post-Truth: Why We Have Reached Peak Bullshit and What We Can Do About It* (New York: Little, Brown, 2017).

32. "Trump Only Knows What's on the Internet," *The Late Show with Stephen Colbert*, March 15, 2016.

33. "The concept of global warming was created by and for the Chinese in order to make U.S. manufacturing non-competitive," Trump tweeted on Nov. 6, 2012, 11:15 a.m.

34. NBC News tweeted video footage of Sanders' reply on Nov. 29, 2017, 8:21 a.m.

35. *Pagella Politica* fact-checked the claim on Oct. 3, 2012.

36. Christopher Ingraham, "19 Times Trump Called Jobs Numbers 'Fake' Before They Made Him Look Good," *Washington Post*, March 10, 2017.

37. "Trump gets annoyed with questions about Obama, ends CBS interview: 'That's enough,'" *Washington Free Beacon*, May 1, 2017.

38. Mantzarlis, "Fact-checking Under President Trump," Poynter Institute, Nov. 10, 2016.

39. Michael P. Lynch, "Trump, Truth and the Power of Contradiction," *New York Times*, May 7, 2016.

40. Jeet Heer, "Trump's Lies Destroy Logic As Well As Truth," *New Republic*, Nov. 28, 2016.

41. The Gallup poll was conducted by telephone Sept. 7–11, 2016, with a random sample of 1,020 adults and a margin of error of plus or minus 4 percentage points. See Art Swift, "Americans' Trust in Mass Media Sinks to New Low," Gallup, Sept. 14, 2016.

42. Andrew Guess, Nyhan and Reifler, "'You're Fake News!' The 2017 Poynter Media Trust Survey," Poynter Institute, Nov. 29, 2017.

43. Kyle Cheney, Isaac Arnsdorf, Daniel Lippman, Daniel Strauss and Brent Griffiths, "Donald Trump's Week of Misrepresentations, Exaggerations and Half-Truths," *Politico Magazine*, Sept. 25, 2016.

44. Davis, Post-Truth, 290.

45. The YouGov/Economist poll was conducted Oct. 15–18, 2016, and surveyed 1,300 people, with a margin of error of plus or minus 3.9

percentage points. (The Economist Group is the parent company of CQ.)

46. Mantzarlis, "Debates Chief Makes Unfortunate Argument Against Fact-Checking," Poynter Institute, Sept. 25, 2016.

47. Mantzarlis, "Rating Lester Holt on the Potted-Plant-O-Meter," Poynter Institute, Sept. 27, 2016.

48. For more suggestions, see Mantzarlis, "Here's How America's Fact-Checkers Would Moderate Tonight's Debate," Poynter Institute, Sept. 26, 2106.

49. Mantzarlis, "Poll: 60 Percent of Americans Want Moderators to Fact-Check the Debate," Poynter Institute, Sept. 26, 2106.

50. Jeffrey Gottfried and Elisa Shearer, "Americans' Online News Use Is Closing in on TV News Use," Pew Research Center, Sept. 7, 2017.

51. Max Read, "Donald Trump Won Because of Facebook," *New York Magazine*, Nov. 9, 2016.

52. James Warren, "Did Fake News Help Elect Trump? Not Likely, According to New Research," Poynter Institute, Jan. 18, 2017.

53. Guess, Nyhan, and Reifler, "Selective Exposure to Misinformation: Evidence From the Consumption of Fake News During the 2016 U.S. Presidential Campaign," Jan. 9, 2018.

54. Mantzarlis, "The More Partisan Your Online Media Diet, the Less Likely You Are to Believe Fact-Checkers," Poynter Institute, Aug. 24, 2016.

55. Lynch, "Fake News and the Internet Shell Game," *New York Times*, Nov. 28, 2016.

56. Michael Barthel and Gottfried, "Majority of U.S. Adults Think News Media Should Not Add Interpretation to the Facts," Pew Research Center, Nov. 18, 2016.

57. Mantzarlis, "Politifact Raised $105,000 in 20 Days Through Its Newly Launched Membership Program," Poynter Institute, Feb. 7, 2017.

58. Daniel Funke, "Want to Be a Better Online Sleuth? Learn to Read Webpages Like a Fact-Checker," Poynter Institute, Oct. 16, 2017.

CHAPTER 8

1.   Kate Starbird, paper prepared for the Association for the Advancement of Artificial Intelligence (pre-print version), 2017.

2.   Faiz Siddiqui and Susan Svrluga, "N.C. Man Told Police He Went to D.C. Pizzeria With Gun to Investigate Conspiracy Theory," *Washington Post*, Dec. 5, 2016.

3.   The online Economist/YouGov poll surveyed 1,376 U.S. adults Dec. 17–20, 2016. (The Economist Group is the parent company of CQ.) Kathy Frankovic summarized the findings of the poll in "Belief in Conspiracies Largely Depends on Political Identity," YouGov, Dec. 27, 2016.

4.   Starbird, "Information Wars: A Window into the Alternative Media Ecosystem," Medium, March 14, 2017.

5.   An overview of the research on attempting to correct false assumptions held by the public can be found in Jesse Singal, "There's (More) Hope for Political Fact-Checking," *The Cut*, Nov. 7, 2016.

6.   According to a survey on news use across social-media platforms conducted by the Pew Research Center in August 2017 (4,971 U.S. adults as respondents). Although the percentage of Americans receiving news from social media is growing fast (up from 62 percent in a Pew survey in 2016), it's important to point out that only 20 percent of the respondents said they do this "often," while 20 percent did this "hardly ever." See Elisa Shearer and Jeffrey Gottfried, "News Use Across Social Media Platforms 2017," Pew Research Center, Sept. 6, 2017.

7.   According to a survey of 4,183 people conducted Nov. 29–Dec. 12, 2016. See Gottfried, Michael Barthel and Amy Mitchell, "Trump, Clinton Divided in Their Main Source for Election News," Pew Research Center, Jan. 18, 2017.

8.   Yochai Benkler, Robert Faris, Hal Roberts and Ethan Zuckerman, "Study: Breitbart-led right-wing media ecosystem altered broader media," *Columbia Journalism Review*, March 3, 2016.

9.   Sarah Oates and Wendy W. Moe, "Donald Trump and the 'Oxygen of Publicity': Branding, Social Media, and Traditional Media," in *The Presidency and Social Media: Discourse, Disruption, and Digital Democracy in the 2016 Presidential Election*, ed. Dan Schill and John Allen Hendricks (New York: Routledge, 2017).

10. In the case of the vaccine/autism conspiracy theory, it is worth noting that the mainstream media were largely responsible for establishing this incorrect conviction with flawed and sensationalist reporting of the original report.

11. For an in-depth discussion of Russian media, please see Chapter 3 of my book, *Revolution Stalled: The Political Limits of the Internet in the Post-Soviet Sphere* (New York: Oxford University Press, 2013).

12. Elizabeth Nelson and Robert Orttung, "Measuring RT's Impact on YouTube," paper presented at the Postcommunist Politics Social Science Workshop, Institute for European, Russian and Eurasian Studies, Elliott School of International Affairs, George Washington University, Washington, D.C., 2013.

13. Bill Chappell, "TV Company Linked to Russia's RT America Registers as Foreign Agent in U.S.," NPR, Nov. 14, 2017.

14. See the 2016 report on Russia's freedom of the press by Freedom House.

15. See *Meduza*'s special report released in December 2017 on recent crackdowns on Russian media by an independent Russian media organization, "A Hybrid Hunt for Criminal Journalists Meduza Reviews How Federal Censors Monitor and Punish Russia's Mass Media."

16. Paul Mozur, "China Spreads Propaganda to U.S. on Facebook, a Platform It Bans at Home," *New York Times*, Nov. 8, 2017.

17. The Washington Post studied a selected sample of social media posts funded by Russian sources. See Dan Keating, Kevin Schaul and Leslie Shapiro, "The Facebook ads Russians targeted at different groups," *Washington Post*, Nov. 1, 2017.

18. Stephen Wilson, "Russian Efforts on Foreign Social Media," paper presented at the Annual Convention of Association for Slavic, East European, and Eurasian Studies, Chicago, Illinois, 2017.

19. Cecilia Kang, "F.C.C. Opens Door to More Consolidation in TV Business," *New York Times*, Nov. 16, 2017.

20. Andrew Chadwick, *The Hybrid Media System: Power and Politics* (New York: Oxford University Press, 2017).

CHAPTER 9

1.   John McCain, "Mr. President, Stop Attacking the Press," *Washington Post*, January 2018.

2.   "Full Text: Jeff Flake on Trump Speech Transcript," *Politico*, Jan. 17, 2018.

3.   "American Views: Trust, Media, and Democracy," Knight Foundation, Jan. 16, 2018. The Gallup/Knight Foundation survey was conducted by mail.

4.   Paul Farhi, "Trump Opens All the Envelopes Himself at First 'Fake News Awards,'" *Washington Post*, Jan. 18, 2018.

5.   Ashley Gold, "Twitter: More Than 677,000 U.S. Users Engaged With Russian Troll Accounts," *Politico*, Jan. 19, 2018.

6.   Adam Mosseri, "Helping Ensure News on Facebook Is From Trusted Sources," Facebook, Jan. 19, 2018.

7.   John F. Kennedy, remarks on the 20th Anniversary of the Voice of America, 1962.

About the Authors

Joshua Benton is director of the Nieman Journalism Lab at Harvard University, a think tank and newsroom that studies and promotes innovation. Before founding the Lab in 2008, he spent 10 years as a reporter, columnist and correspondent for newspapers, most recently at The Dallas Morning News. His investigative reports on cheating on standardized tests in the Texas public schools led to the permanent shutdown of a school district and won the Philip Meyer Journalism Award from Investigative Reporters and Editors. He has been a fellow at Harvard (2007), Johns Hopkins University (2003), and the East-West Center (2005) and currently serves on the boards of The Hechinger Report at Columbia University and the International Reporting Project at New America. He is a lecturer at Boston University, a regular panelist on WGBH's "Beat the Press" and has spoken about journalism issues in more than a dozen countries around the world. He is a graduate of Yale University.

Katherine K. Ellis is a program associate at the American Press Institute, focusing primarily on diversity initiatives and marketing outreach. She has had internships at the American Copy Editors Society, Bloglovin', USA Today Network-Wisconsin and, most recently, NPR's Next Generation Radio. She worked at The Daily Utah Chronicle for four years, her final year as editor-in-chief. She graduated from the University of Utah, having majored in journalism, marketing and public relations.

Jonas Kaplan is a cognitive neuroscientist whose research uses functional magnetic resonance imaging to study the cognitive and social aspects of brain function. He is assistant professor (research) of psychology at the University of Southern California's Brain and Creativity Institute and in the Department of Psychology. Kaplan serves as the co-director of the Dornsife Cognitive Neuroimaging Center at USC. His research has targeted a wide range of neural systems, including investigations into the neural systems that underlie empathy, self-awareness, political and social identity. Kaplan also uses machine learning approaches combined with neuroimaging to understand multisensory integration and concept formation in the brain. Kaplan's recent work has explored the neural basis of deeply held values and beliefs, with the goal of understanding how the brain's systems for identity and meaning-making shape who we are.

Kaplan earned a B.S. in psychology at the University of Michigan and a Ph.D. in cognitive neuroscience from the University of California Los Angeles.

Matt Mansfield is a former senior vice president at CQ Roll Call and was the company's first chief innovation officer. He's now a partner in Mansfield/Goldman Strategy, whose client roster includes the National Governors Association, USA Football and Agency Q.

He was in charge of both Congressional Quarterly's and Roll Call's user experience and product development.

Previously, Mansfield was executive editor, digital at National Geographic, an associate professor at Northwestern University's Medill School of Journalism and the co-director of the school's program in Washington, D.C., and a deputy managing editor of the San Jose Mercury News. He was president and annual workshop chair for the Society for News Design and was one of the longtime D.C. organizers for the Online News Association's monthly meet-ups and was program co-chair for ONA's annual conference in Chicago.

Alexios Mantzarlis is director of the International Fact-Checking Network, a global forum for fact-checking organizations launched in September 2015 based at the Poynter Institute for Media Studies. In this capacity he writes about fact-checking and trains fact-checkers around the world. He helped draft the fact-checkers' code of principles, a set of guiding standards for fact-checking initiatives, and helped launch International Fact-Checking Day. In late 2015, he shepherded a partnership between third-party fact-checkers and Facebook that resulted in a pilot project to flag fake news on the social media platform. He has spoken at premier conferences for journalism around the world, including at the International Journalism Festival, the International Symposium on Online Journalism and South by Southwest. Mantzarlis previously served as managing editor of Pagella Politica and FactCheckEU, Italy's main political fact-checking website and the EU's first multilingual crowd-checking project.

Previously, he worked for the United Nations and the Italian Institute for International Political Studies. Mantzarlis holds a B.A. in philosophy, politics and economics from the University of York, a M.A. in European affairs from the Institut d'Etudes Politiques de Paris and a M.S. in economics and management from Bocconi University in Milan.

Bryan Monroe is the Verizon chair and professor at Temple University's Klein College of Media and Communication, where he leads courses in media, innovation entrepreneurship and social change. Before joining Temple, he was the Washington editor, opinion & commentary at CNN and the editor of CNNPolitics.com. His work included editorial planning and content strategy across all online platforms in its Washington bureau. He previously served as assistant vice president of news at Knight Ridder Newspapers, where he helped lead journalists at the Biloxi Sun Herald to the 2006 Pulitzer Prize Gold Medal for Public Service for their coverage of Hurricane Katrina. Monroe was also vice president and editorial director at "EBONY" and "Jet" magazines, where he led coverage of the 2008 presidential election.

Monroe has a B.A. from the University of Washington and was a Nieman fellow at Harvard University. He has been a visiting professor at Northwestern University's Medill School of Journalism and was president of the National Association of Black Journalists from 2005 to 2007. He is also the managing director of Monroe Media Group, a Washington-based media strategy, crisis communications and personal branding company.

Sarah Oates is professor and senior scholar at the Philip Merrill College of Journalism at the University of Maryland, College Park. A former journalist, she is a political communication professor with 25 years of experience in analyzing media production, content and audiences. A major theme in her work is the way in which the traditional media and the internet can support or subvert democracy. She has published many books, articles, chapters, and papers on topics ranging from how the internet can challenge dictatorships, the way election coverage varies in different countries and how national media systems cover terrorism in distinctive ways. Her most recent book, "Revolution Stalled: The Political Limits of the Internet in the Post-Soviet Sphere," won the Alex Nove Prize in Russian, Soviet and Post-Soviet Studies from the British Association for Slavonic and East European Studies. Her current work examines how political messages travel through media ecosystems.

Along with colleagues in Maryland's Computer Science Department, Oates is working on a software application to improve synergy between human coders and machine learning in understanding how narratives travel in the online sphere. She regularly comments on politics for the BBC and other media. Oates earned a Ph.D. in political science from Emory University and is a Fulbright alumna.

Tom Rosenstiel is executive director of the American Press Institute. Previously, he was founder and, for 16 years, director of the Project for Excellence in Journalism at Pew Research Center and co-founder and vice chair of the Committee of Concerned Journalists. He is also a nonresident senior fellow at the Brookings Institution. His first novel, "Shining City," was published in February 2017. Rosenstiel is the author of seven nonfiction books, including "The Elements of Journalism: What News People Should Know and the Public Should Expect," which has been translated into more than 25 languages and won the Goldsmith Book Award from Harvard University. He and Bill Kovach have written two other books together, including "Blur: How to Know What's True in the Age of Information Overload." "The New Ethics of Journalism: Principles for the 21st Century," was co-edited with Kelly McBride of the Poynter Institute in 2013.

He worked as media writer for the Los Angeles Times for a decade, chief congressional correspondent for Newsweek, press critic for MSNBC, business editor of the Peninsula Times Tribune and as a reporter for Jack Anderson's "Washington Merry Go 'Round" column. Among his awards are four Sigma Delta Chi Awards for Journalism Research. He has a B.A. from Oberlin College and a M.S. from the Columbia School of Journalism.

Frank Sesno is director of George Washington University's School of Media and Public Affairs, where he leads a faculty of nearly two dozen who research and teach journalism, political communication and the impact of digital media in international affairs. Sesno is an internationally recognized journalist with more than 30 years of experience reporting from around the world. He joined CNN in 1984 and for seven years was White House correspondent, after which he moved to the anchor chair. From 1996 through 2001, he served as the Washington bureau chief and senior vice president. For seven years, he hosted "Late Edition with Frank Sesno," CNN's flagship weekend interview program.

In 2017, Sesno published a book, "Ask More: The Power of Questions to Open Doors, Uncover Solutions, and Spark Change," illustrating that what connects the world's most successful people is that they ask the right questions at the right time. Sesno graduated cum laude with a B.A. in American History from Middlebury College. He was conferred an Honorary Doctorate of humane letters in 1995 by the Monterrey Institute of International Studies in California and two honorary doctorates by his alma mater, Middlebury, in 2009 and Eckerd College in 2017.

Ellen Shearer is the William F. Thomas professor in the Medill School of Journalism, Media, Integrated Marketing Communications at Northwestern University and executive editor of the school's Washington Program, Medill News Service. She also is co-director of the Medill National Security Journalism initiative. She is co-author of the book "Nonvoters: America's No-Shows," created and edited, with colleagues, "Whistleblowers, Leaks and the Media" and "National Security Law in the News: A Guide for Journalists, Scholars and Policymakers," both published by the American Bar Association Publishing; wrote chapters for six books on journalism; and produced a five-lecture online curriculum, "The James W. Foley Guide on Journalists' Safety."

Before joining the Medill faculty, she was a senior editor at New York Newsday, a consulting editor at Newhouse News Service, marketing executive at Reuters and held positions as senior executive, bureau chief and reporter during a 10-year stint at United Press International. Shearer is past president of the Washington Press Club Foundation and since 1999 has coordinated judging for the White House Correspondents' Association's annual awards. She served as an accreditor for the Accrediting Council on Education in Journalism and Mass Communications. She is secretary of the James W. Foley Legacy Foundation. Shearer has a B.A. in communications from the University of Wisconsin and a M.S. in interactive journalism from American University.

Michael Shermer is the founding publisher of "Skeptic" magazine, a monthly columnist for "Scientific American" and presidential fellow at Chapman University. He is the author of "Heavens on Earth," "The Moral Arc," "The Believing Brain," "Why People Believe Weird Things," "Why Darwin Matters," "The Mind of the Market," "How We Believe" and "The Science of Good and Evil." He has been a college professor since 1979, having also taught at Occidental College, Glendale College and Claremont Graduate University. He regularly contributes opinion-editorials, book reviews and essays to The Wall Street Journal, The Los Angeles Times, Science, Nature and other publications. Shermer received his B.A. in psychology from Pepperdine University, M.A. in experimental psychology from California State University, Fullerton and his Ph.D. in the history of science from Claremont Graduate University. He has appeared on such shows as "The Colbert Report," "20/20," "Dateline," "Charlie Rose" and "Larry King Live." His two TED talks, seen by nearly 8 million people, were voted in the top 100 of the more than 2,000 TED talks, after which he delivered a TED All Star talk.

CQ

CQ's software solutions help government relations professionals get more done. These include news and policy analysis and tools for legislative tracking, grassroots advocacy and advocate and donor acquisition.

Roll Call reports on the people and politics of Capitol Hill. Since 1955, its trusted, objective, and non-partisan coverage has been a DC mainstay.

CQ Roll Call is made up of two of the most respected companies in Washington. Our award-winning journalism and state-of-the-art software are relied on by associations, nonprofits, law and lobbying firms, media companies, the U.S. Senate, House of Representatives, Supreme Court and government agencies. CQ Roll Call's parent, The Economist, is the leading source of analysis on international business and world affairs.